AF600412

CANONICAL PROVISIONS FOR UNIVERSITIES AND COLLEGES

THE CATHOLIC UNIVERSITY OF AMERICA
CANON LAW STUDIES
NO. 373

Canonical Provisions for Universities and Colleges

A HISTORICAL SYNOPSIS AND A COMMENTARY

A DISSERTATION

SUBMITTED TO THE FACULTY OF THE SCHOOL OF CANON LAW OF THE CATHOLIC UNIVERSITY OF AMERICA IN PARTIAL FULFILLMENT OF THE REQUIREMENTS FOR THE DEGREE OF DOCTOR OF CANON LAW

BY THE
REV. ALEXANDER F. SOKOLICH, A.B., S.T.L., J.C.L.
PRIEST OF THE ARCHDIOCESE OF NEWARK

THE CATHOLIC UNIVERSITY OF AMERICA PRESS
WASHINGTON, D. C.
1956

NIHIL OBSTAT:

CLEMENS V. BASTNAGEL, S.T.L., J.U.D.
Censor Deputatus

Washingtonii, die 28. apr. 1956

IMPRIMATUR:

✠ THOMAS A. BOLAND, S.T.D.
Archiepiscopus Novarcensis

Novarci, die 30. apr. 1956

Printed by THEO. GAUS' SONS, INC., *Brooklyn* 1, *N. Y., U. S. A.*

DEDICATED TO

MY FATHER AND MOTHER

AND TO THE MEMORY OF THE

VERY REV. MSGR. JOHN J. TIERNEY

TABLE OF CONTENTS

Foreword ix

PART I

HISTORICAL SYNOPSIS

Chapter I

The Origins of and the Legislation for Catholic Universities and Colleges 3

Article 1. The Origins and Growth of Catholic Universities and Colleges in Europe and in the United States of America 3

Section 1. Europe 3
- A. The University of Salerno 5
- B. The University of Bologna 7
- C. The University of Paris 12
- D. The University of Oxford 15
- E. Colleges 17

Section 2. The United States of America 20

Article 2. Positive Legislation—The Middle Ages to the Present 24

Chapter II

The Reformation and the Growth of Non-Catholic Universities and Colleges 30

Article 1. The Growth in Europe 30

Article 2. The Growth in the United States of America 35

CHAPTER III

GENERAL AND SPECIAL LEGISLATION CONCERNING THE ATTENDANCE OF CATHOLICS AT NON-CATHOLIC UNIVERSITIES AND COLLEGES 41

Article 1. The Middle Ages to the Council of Trent (1545-1563) 41

Article 2. The Council of Trent to the III Plenary Council of Baltimore (1884) 44

PART II

CANONICAL COMMENTARY

CHAPTER IV

THE PRESENT PROHIBITION 67

Article 1. The Term *Pueri* and Its Meaning in the Field of Higher Education 67

Article 2. The Meaning of Non-Catholic Universities and Colleges (*Acatholica, Neutra, Mixta*) 78

Article 3. The Penalties 83

CHAPTER V

THE PRESENT TOLERATION 88

Article 1. The Nature of the Term "Toleration" 88

Article 2. The Powers of the Local Ordinary 93

Section 1. *Peregrini* 98

Section 2. Clerics and Women Religious 105

Section 3. Vigilance and Visitation 111

Section 4. Delegation 118

Article 3. The Instructions of the Holy See.............. 120
Section 1. Circumstances 136
Section 2. Safeguards 138

Article 4. The Decree of the Local Ordinary 139

CHAPTER VI

THE ATTENDANCE OF NON-CATHOLICS AT CATHOLIC UNIVERSITIES AND COLLEGES 145

Article 1. The Proportionate Number of Non-Catholics who May Be Permitted to Attend Catholic Universities and Colleges 151

Article 2. The Religious Instruction of Non-Catholics Who Attend Catholic Universities and Colleges 157

CONCLUSIONS 164

BIBLIOGRAPHY 166

ALPHABETICAL INDEX 174

BIOGRAPHICAL NOTE 180

FOREWORD

This work is the result of the writer's attempt to accomplish a double purpose. In the Church's exercise of the teaching function required of it by the divine mandate of its Founder, Jesus Christ, it is important, first, to see that there will be problems. The popes have seen them and have tried to focus attention on them. That is the first objective of this dissertation, namely, to focus attention on the problems. The popes in their own messages, and through the Instructions of the administrative agencies of the Church, the Sacred Congregations, and through the laws incorporated in the Code of Canon Law, have provided the general solutions. The norms for particular solutions to problems which have accidental variations by reason of circumstances are available to local ordinaries from the law of the Church and from the Instructions of the Holy See. That is the second objective of this discussion, namely, to point out the applications of the law of the Church to some of the problems.

The scope of the discussion is a limited one. There is a treatment of education on the university and college levels only, and of only particular elements in that broad field. The *Historical Synopsis* will place before the reader the origins of Catholic universities and colleges and the early legislation of the Church with regard to Catholic universities and colleges. It will also advert to the problems created by the attendance of Catholics at non-Catholic universities and colleges during and after the Reformation.

In the *Canonical Commentary,* the nature of the present law which governs the attendance of Catholics at universities and colleges of a neutral or a mixed character is inspected along with the allied question of non-Catholic students in relation to Catholic universities and colleges.

It is the prayerful hope of the writer that superior theological and legal minds will be attracted to a study of the problems in education on the university and college levels, particularly in the United States.

The writer welcomes this occasion to express his sincere gratitude to His Excellency, the Most Reverend Thomas A. Boland, S. T. D., the Archbishop of Newark, for the opportunity of advanced study in Canon Law at the Catholic University of America. The writer wishes also to thank the Rev. Francis J. Connell, C.SS.R. for his kind encouragement, the Reverend Clement V. Bastnagel, J.U.D., for his generous and scholarly guidance, the Faculty of the School of Canon Law, his classmates, and all others whose helpful suggestions have made this dissertation possible.

PART I

HISTORICAL SYNOPSIS

CHAPTER I

THE ORIGINS OF THE LEGISLATION FOR CATHOLIC UNIVERSITIES AND COLLEGES.

Article 1. The Origins and Growth of Catholic Universities and Colleges in Europe and in the United States of America.

Section 1. Europe.

The gradual establishment and growth of universities in the XII century prompts one to look for the causes of a movement which has lasted through the centuries. The Crusades; the renewal of enthusiasm for things philosophical; the emergence of free, ambitious, independent city-states; the impetus to the desire for study in practical fields given by the need for lawyers and doctors; the imperial and papal power and patronage for the founding of schools, so that men might be trained for living their lives as creatures of God destined one day to return to Him—these are assigned by historians of education as causes for the development of the medieval universities.[1]

The term university, *universitas,* which at present is applied to an institution for the teaching or the cultivation of universal knowledge, had not that meaning in the Middle Ages. The notion of a university as an *universitas facultatum* or as a school in which all the faculties or branches of knowledge are represented is of much more recent origin. When, in papal documents, the words *universitas vestra* were used, they meant simply "all of you."[2] In the technical sense of Roman Law, the term *universitas*

---

[1] McCormick and Cassidy, *History of Education* (Washington, D.C., The Catholic Education Press, 1953), pp. 280, 281.

[2] Wernz, *Ius Decretalium* (6 vols., Prati, 1898-1914), III (1901), nn. 83 ff.

was practically the equivalent of *collegium,* a legal corporation, or a moral person, or a community.[3]

When at the end of the XII century the term did begin to be applied to schools, it was always applied to the scholastic body of either the teachers or the scholars. It had no reference, at that time, to the place in which such a body was established nor even to its collective schools. Thus the term meant the "Corporation of Teachers" or the "Corporation of Students." When the corporation was made up of teachers and students it constituted an *universitas magistrorum et scholarium.* The newly formed Guilds and Municipalities used the same term (*universitas*) in speaking of their legally constituted associations. The corporation aggregate by which any particular school was maintained was the *universitas* of the Middle Ages. Thus, in Bologna, where the term was first used, the students constituted the corporation, elected the rector, engaged the professors and conducted the affairs of the school.[4]

The term *studium* was the word used to designate the academic institution. Thus the references to resident students were made in the following manner: *in studio degere* or *in scholis militare.* The indefinite notion of a university as an institution for higher education as distinguished from a mere school, seminary, or some private establishment for instruction, finds some correspondence in the term *studium generale,* which did not become common until the XIII century. Even this term, however, had not the meaning of a place where all subjects were studied, but rather a place where students from all countries were received. Although the meaning of *studium generale* remained somewhat vague, it seems to have implied, in the XIII century, three main characteristics; (1) that the school invited and attracted students from all lands, and not merely those of a particular country or district; (2) that it was a place of higher education, i.e., at least one of the higher

---

[3] *Codex Iuris Canonici,* Pii X Pontificis Maximi iussu digestus, Benedicti XV auctoritate promulgatus (Romae: Typis Polyglottis Vaticanis, 1917; reimpressio, 1934), Can. 100, §§ 1, 2.

[4] Moore, *The Story of Instruction* (New York, The Macmillan Company, 1938), p. 334; Cicognani, *Canon Law* (2. ed., Reprint, Westminster, Maryland: The Newman Press, 1949), pp. 268, 269.

branches of learning such as theology, law or medicine was taught there, and (3) that such subjects were taught by a number of masters.[5]

Three *studia* enjoyed great prestige at the beginning of the XIII century. They were Salerno for medicine, Bologna for law and Paris for theology and arts. A Master who had taught and been admitted to the Magisterial Guild of one of these places was certain of obtaining immediate recognition and permission in all other *Studia,* but these *Studia* themselves did not receive Masters from other schools without a previous examination. The listing is chronological, and in that order a brief conspectus of the origins and constitutions of these *Studia* will be given, since so many of the European universities claim one or the other as their own Mother-University. A brief summary of the origins of Oxford will follow these.

A. The University of Salerno.

The early history of Salerno begins with Constantinus Africanus. A native of Carthage, he wandered throughout the East. After his return to Carthage, he fled to Salerno to avoid the invasion of the Norman, Robert Guiscard. Eventually he retired to the Abbey of Monte Cassino, where under the famous Abbot Desiderius, afterwards Pope Victor III (1086-1087), he occupied himself for the remainder of his life in making Latin translations or compilations from Arabic or Greek medical writers.[6]

---

[5] Chronicle of Eno (c. 1190) : "In tempore illo fuit clericus adolescens, praefati fundatoris amite filius et nomine equivocus (magister Eno), qui a primis puericiae suae annis litteralibus fuit studiis imbutus. Is cum fuisset in limine adolescentiae suae, et ipse parvulus parvulos imbueret apud quosdam beati Benedicti religosos . . . Qui cum mare versus Angliam anno aetatis suae quasi 20 transiisset communis causa studii litterarum, quod fuit Oxoniae, aestuabat uberius liberalibus artibus se implicare."—*Monumenta Germaniae Historica, Scriptores,* Inde ab Anno Christi Quingentesimo usque ad Annum Millesimum et Quingentesimum, Tom. XXIII (ed. Georgius Heinricus Pertz, Hannoverae, 1874), p. 467 (hereafter cited *MGH, Scriptores*) ; Hostiensis (Henricus de Segusio), *In Decretalium Libros Commentaria* (5 vols. in 3, Venetiis, 1581), Lib. V, Tit. V, c. 5.

[6] *MGH, Scriptores,* VII, 728. The historical controversy over Constantinus' identity and influence in the beginnings of the Medical School

His translation from the Arabic of the "Aphorisms of Hippocrates" was produced at Monte Cassino about the year 1080. This text remained a basic one for many years in the medical schools. He followed this with the works of Galen. By 1099 an organized school or college of doctors existed at Salerno. It has not been claimed that Salerno was ever a regular university. Certainly there was no university of students. The college of doctors made it at best a forerunner of the Parisian type of university. Essentially Salerno was a medical school, where a number of subjects relating to the study and practice of medicine were taught. Thus a student was required to study for three years *in scientia logicali* as an indispensable aid for his study of medicine. The course in medicine consisted of lectures on Hippocrates (5th-4th cent., B. C.) and Galen (2nd cent.). This, in turn, was followed by a year of practice *cum consilio experti medici.*[7]

In 1231 Salerno was given its first official recognition by Emperor Frederick II (1212-1250). The imperial approbation came, however, only after Frederick had required of all who were to teach or practice medicine a Royal License, which he granted only after an examination in the Emperor's Court. These examinations were to be conducted by the Masters of Salerno and certain other Royal Officers.[8]

In 1253 an attempt was made to add other Faculties to the School of Medicine at Salerno, but by 1258 it became obvious that the experiment had failed at Salerno, and it became again a School of Medicine only.[9]

For two centuries Salerno's position as a School of Medicine was as unique as that of Paris in theology and that of Bologna in

---

at Salerno is carefully catalogued by Hastings Rashdall in *The Universities of Europe in the Middle Ages* (3 vols., ed. F. M. Powicke and A. B. Emden, Oxford: The Clarendon Press, 1936), I, 76 ff. (hereafter cited Rashdall).

[7] Huillard-Breholles, *Historia Diplomatica Frederici II* (7 vols. in 12, Parisiis, excudebant Plon Fratres, 1852-1861), IV (1855), 235, 236 (hereafter cited *Historia Diplomatica*).

[8] *Historia Diplomatica,* II (1852), 149, 150.

[9] *Ibidem,* pp. 447-453.

law. Throughout the Middle Ages no School of Medicine rivaled its fame, except, perhaps, Montpellier.[10]

B. The University of Bologna.

The revival of intellectual activity in Italy had a close relationship with the victory of the Lombard League at Legnano in 1176 and the Treaty of Constance in 1183. As the Lombard cities awoke to a consciousness of their recovered liberty, they turned their energies to political life, while the areas north of the Alps were taken up with the revival of metaphysical and theological speculation and the rediscovery of Aristotle. The society of the Italian cities was commercial and political, and the demands centered about a practical knowledge or science which could be applied to the regulation of social life. This demand was met through a revival of the study of the long-neglected, but never wholly forgotten, monuments of Roman Jurisprudence. In such communities, then, the Science of Law awakened great intellectual enthusisam. In such communities, too, the democratic institution of a University of Students could spring into existence. Such a university grew in Bologna.[11]

The Civil Law movement did not begin in Bologna any more than did the Scholastic movement begin in Paris. There were Schools of Law before Bologna's rise, v.g., at Rome, Pavia and Ravenna. In fact, the earliest fame of Bologna was that of a School of the Liberal Arts. By the year 1000 it was already sufficiently famous as a *Studium* of Arts to attract St. Guido, afterward Bishop of Aqui (1035-1070), from a region as distant as the neighborhood of Genoa.[12] St. Bruno, Bishop of Segni (d. 1123), was also a student of the Liberal Arts at Bologna.[13]

---

[10] Denifle, *Die Entstehung der Universitäten des Mittelalters bis* 1400 (Berlin, 1885), p. 233 (hereafter cited Denifle).

[11] Rashdall, I, 98.

[12] *Acta Sanctorum* (71 vols., Parisiis, 1863-1940), Jun., T. I (1867), 229: "Abeunte igitur aetate Guido memoratus . . . studiorum causa Bononiae contendit. Ubi aliquot annis non minus sanctis moribus quam litterarum disciplinam incumbens socios et aemulatores sui in utroque studii honore devicit."

[13] *Ibidem,* Jul. T. IV (1868), 479.

The influence of two men was indeed very great in the rise of Bologna. Irnerius (d. 1138), who taught there in the years between 1100 and 1130, was the first to lecture on the whole collection of the *Digesta.* It was also in his time that a systematic, philosophical study of the whole *Corpus Iuris Civilis* became the regular curriculum of an ordinary legal education. Such a schedule required the full and undivided attention of a student. Thus no student of the Arts could venture into such a vast and technical field until his School education was completed.[14] Gratian, meanwhile, was compiling his *Decretum,*[15] by reediting all the materials collected by a succession of canonists.[16] With the appearance of the *Decretum* at Bologna, the schools had a textbook of Ecclesiastical Law. It was quickly recognized as such. Gratian's object was to extract from the conflict of opinions the doctrine which from its superior authority, its more recent date, its intrinsic reasonableness could be taken for the doctrine of the Church. It was the acceptance and use of Gratian's *Decretum* as a textbook that was to bring about the separation of Canon Law from Theology as a particular field of study, so that the former was no longer to be considered merely as a small, undefined branch of Theology.[17]

From this time the distinction of the teachers and the students of law from other students and teachers came to be much more sharply drawn, and extended itself to all universities and schools at which law was taught at all. In the light of the required, previ-

[14] Rashdall, I, 118-127; Cicognani, *Canon Law,* pp. 271, 272.

[15] The exact time of the publication of the *Decretum* is the subject of much controversy. It may be concluded that it certainly appeared before 1143. A.M. Stickler, in his *Historia Iuris Canonici Latini,* I, *Historia Fontium* (Augustae Taurinorum: Apud Custodiam Librariam Pontif. Athenaii Salesiani, 1950), on p. 204 writes: "Opus (*Decretum*) ergo a. 1140, ad summum inter a. 1140-42 est adornatum et absolutum."

[16] Among his more important predecessors were Burchard of Worms (*Decretum* [1012-1023]), Anselm of Lucca (*Collectio Canonum* [ca. 1083]), and Cardinal Deusdedit (*Collectio Canonum* [ca. 1083-1086]).

[17] Sarti, *De Claris Archygymnasii Bononiensis professoribus a saeculo XI usque ad saeculum XIV* (2 vols., Bononiae, Ex Typographis Laelii a Vulpe Instituti Scientiarum Typographi, 1769-72—completed by Fattorini after Sarti's death), I, pt. 1, p. 273 (hereafter cited Sarti).

ous preparation and the division of Law as constituting simply a branch of Rhetoric, the character and the class of students also changed. Older and more independent men made their way to Bologna. This occasioned an evolution in the University system in what was the most characteristic institution of Bologna, namely, the Student-University. It would be a misconception, however, to conclude that Bologna became, during the work of Irnerius and Gratian, a School of Law and nothing more. Bologna still retained its character as an institution where general literary studies were taught.[18]

The Student-University idea, in its origins, grew because of the many non-Bolognese students. Their need, as non-citizens, for co-operation and mutual protection moved the many foreign students at Bologna to form their own Student Guilds.[19]

The professors were excluded from membership in the student guilds simply because they were citizens of Bologna and already had political status. It was also the practice among foreign merchants and other strangers in Italian cities to form themselves into guilds for the preventing of quarrels among themselves and the promotion of their common interests.[20]

The Statutes of the German Guild of Students, still preserved, indicate the original purpose and organization of the Student-Universities.

> "Haec nostra congregatio, utilitatis tamen publice et private nequaquam expers credenda, praesertim ex qua fraterna caritas, societatis amicitieque communicatio, informorum consolatio et egenorum subsidium, funerum deductio et rancoris simultatumque extirpatio, tum doctorandorum nostrorum in locum et ex loco examinis comitia atque constipacio, bona spiritualia resultarent."[21]

---

[18] *MGH, Scriptores,* XVIII, 639.

[19] The words of Pope Honorius III (1216-1227), to the Tuscans and Campanians makes this point clear: "Etsi multam honestatem immo necessitatem, sicut asseritis, causa contineat, quae vos ad contrahendam societatem induxit."—Sarti, II, 58.

[20] Denifle, p. 136.

[21] Rashdall, I, 160, note 1.

From the time of his matriculation[22] to the time of his graduation, the student attended at least three two-hour lectures daily.[23] The lectures were given in the homes of the *Doctors* or in some rented public buildings. Savigny (1779-1861)[24] gives the following account of a course of lectures:

> "First, I shall give you summaries of each Title before I proceed to the text; secondly, I shall give you as clear and explicit a statement as I can of the purport of each Law included in the Title; thirdly, I shall read the text with a view to correcting it; fourthly, I shall repeat the contents of the Law; fifthly, I shall solve apparent contradictions, adding any general principles of Law (*Brocardica*), and any distinctions or subtle and useful problems (*Quaestiones*) arising out of the Law with their solutions as far as Divine Providence enables me."

The lectures at Bologna were in conversational style and the Statutes required that the *Glossae* be read immediately after the text.[25] In Lent, all extra classes and sessions held by the *Doctors* were suspended, and student Disputations were held in their place.[26] After five years of study a student of Civil Law could be admitted by the Rector to lecture on a single Title. A canonist, similarly, could lecture on a single Title after four years of study.[27] The end of the next year of study, after an examination,

---

[22] The placing of the name of the student on the *Matricula* or list of members of the university was, originally, peculiar to the Student-Universities, for only in them was the student a full member of the university. Cf. Denifle, *Archiv für Literatur und Kirchengeschichte* (7 vols., Berlin, 1885-1889), III, 128 ff. (hereafter cited *Statuta,* since the Statutes of Bologna are collected in the third volume of the work).

[23] *Statuta,* p. 105.

[24] *Geschichte des römischen Rechts im Mittelalter* (7 vols., Heidelberg; J.C.B. Mohr, 1834-1851; Nachdruck, 1934-1935, I, Cap. XXIII, § 204.

[25] *Statuta,* p. 105.

[26] *Statuta,* p. 106.

[27] *Statuta,* p. 111.

made the student eligible for the *Licentia docendi,* and after his final year of successful study he could apply for the Doctorate.[28]

The process of graduation consisted of two parts, i.e., the Private Examination and the Public Examination. The latter was, in practice, a ceremony only. The candidate's fitness was proved in the Private Examination. The candidate was presented to the Rector, who along with two *Doctors* presented him to the Archdeacon. After attending a Mass in honor of the Holy Ghost, the candidate appeared before the assembled *Collegium* and was assigned by one of the *Doctors* two passages (*puncta*) in Civil or Canon Law, as the case might be.[29] Later in the day the candidate, in the presence of the *Collegium* and the Archdeacon, gave an exposition of the two passages. He was questioned on the involved points of law by two *Doctors* appointed by the *Collegium.* The other Doctors were free to ask supplementary questions or to raise objections to the candidate's answers. The examination concluded, the votes of the Doctors were taken up and the decision of the majority was announced by the Archdeacon.[30]

The position and the importance of the Archdeacon is evident from what has been said above. The authority of the Archdeacon was established by Pope Honorius III in 1219. He had himself been the Archdeacon of Bologna, and he ordered that no Doctorate could be granted without the consent of the Archdeacon, who was the Head of the Chapter School. By this Bull and the imitation of its provisions throughout the other Universities of Europe, all Universities were brought under the control of the Church. It came to be a recognized requirement of every University organization that it should have an official duly constituted by ecclesiastical authority. In 1292, Pope Nicholas IV conferred on all Doctors licensed by the Archdeacon of Bologna the right to teach throughout the whole world.[31] The Archdeacon occupied, with respect to the University of Bologna, the same position as did the Chancellor of the Cathedral with the University of Paris. Origin-

[28] *Statuta,* p. 113.

[29] Statuta, pp. 116-119,

[30] *Statuta,* pp. 384, 385.

[31] Sarti, T. I, pt. 2, pp. 59, 60.

ally the Archdeacon or Chancellor was not an official or even a member *ex officio* of either the University of Students or the University of Masters. Thus, if a Doctor of the School of Canon Law received the appointment of Archdeacon, he ceased to be a member of the School, unless by way of a special dispensation he was retained through a unanimous vote.[32] He was the representative of the Church's authority over the *Studium Generale.* It was under the Chancellor[33] that universities passed from local into ecumenical organizations, so that the Doctorate became an order of intellectual nobility with as distinct and definte a place in the Middle Ages as the Priesthood or the Knighthood.

C. The University of Paris.

This University was the outgrowth of the Cathedral School of Paris. The educational activity was transferred from the monks to the secular clergy. In this change were the beginnings of the University movement at Paris.[34] William of Champeaux (1070-1121) at the Cathedral, Abelard (1079-1142) at St. Genevieve and Adam (d. 1192) and Hugh (1096-1141) and Walter (d. end of 12th cent.) of St. Victor attracted great numbers of students to their lectures. As the numbers increased, their presence in Paris required a multiplication of teachers or Masters.[35] As the number of Masters grew, it was not long before the need of some authority to evaluate the qualifications of the Masters became apparent. Stephen of Tournay (1128-1203) complained of the extreme youth and the profane audacity of some of the Masters who had gathered scholars around themselves.[36]

Sometime in the XII century the practice of making each Master of the Schools a regular member of the Cathedral Body was

---

[32] *Statuta,* p. 343.

[33] "Universitatem Studii Bononiae, cui archdiaconatum ipsum pro tempore obtinens, ut illius major Cancellarius, praeesse dignoscitur." *Statuta,* p. 417.

[34] Migne, *Patrologiae Cursus Completus, Series Latina* (221 vols., Parisiis, 1844-1864, CXLV, 621 (hereafter cited *MPL*).

[35] Denifle, pp. 656 ff.

[36] *MPL,* CCXI, 517.

introduced. The III General Council of the Lateran (1179) required that those who sought to set themselves up as Masters acquire a formal permission or license to teach from the Masters of the Church Schools. It forbade the Masters to accept any fee or gift for granting the *licentia docendi,* and they were required to grant the license to every properly qualified applicant.[37] The IV General Council of the Lateran (1215) repeated the injunctions of the previous Lateran Council, and insisted that each Metropolitan Church should also have a *Theologus.*[38]

With the legislation on licenses and the intellectual enthusiasm of the age, it was not too long before Paris became almost a city of teachers. The Cathedral and Abbey schools found it impossible to contain the number of students and Masters. The formal induction of a new Master through the *Principium* or *Inceptio*[39] was but a step, even though imperceptible at the time, to the formation of another Trades-Union, that of teachers. The formative period of Paris as a Master-University is placed in the years between 1150-1170. By 1208 the University had written Statutes and was sending legates to the Holy See,[40] and the granting of the *licentia docendi* was under the control of the Chancellor of the University. The emergence of the system whereby a Rector, as an elected official, whose first work looked to the collecting of money for University purposes, the moderating of University litigation, and the executing of University decrees, became actually the head of the whole University, as also the appearance in history of Deans to help the Rector, is carefully investigated by Rashdall (1848-1924).[41]

---

[37] Mansi, *Sacrorum Conciliorum Nova et Amplissima Collectio* (53 vols. in 59, Parisiis, Arnhemii, Lipsiae, 1901-1927), XXII, 228 (hereafter cited Mansi).

[38] Mansi, XXII, 999.

[39] The idea of *Inceptio* involved two elements, i.e., the formal entrance of a newly licensed teacher upon his functions by delivering his inaugural lecture with other Masters present, and entertaining his new colleagues at a banquet. Cf. Gross, *The Gild-Merchant* (Oxford, The Clarendon Press, 1890), pp. 33, 34.

[40] *MPL,* CCXI, 471.

[41] *The Universities of Europe in the Middle Ages,* I, 322-334.

The studies at Paris were not confined to Theology and philosophy. The earliest Statute (ca. 1270-1278) of the Faculty of the School of Medicine at Paris required 32 months of study for the degree of Bachelor, and 5½ years of study for a License in the case of one who had already been licensed in Arts. Otherwise, the student had to spend six years in the study of Medicine before he could be awarded a license.[42] Canon Law was also studied at Paris, but never in the scientific spirit which characterized the Law School at Bologna.

The curriculum of studies required for a Master's degree in Arts comes down to us from the statutes drawn up by the papal legate, Robert de Courçon (d. 1219), in 1215.[43] The course for a Doctorate in Theology extended over a period of eight years in the Statutes of 1215.[44] The Statutes of 1366 extended the complete course over a period of sixteen years.[45] The Faculty, however, enjoyed and employed liberal powers of dispensation. Religious Orders had papal privileges curtailing the period of study

---

[42] Denifle-Chatelain, *Chartularium Universitatis Parisiensis. Sub auspiciis Consilii generalis facultatum Parisiensium ex diversis bibliothecis tabulariisque collegit et cum authenticis chartis contulit Henricus Denifle . . . auxiliante . . . Aemilio Chatelain* (4 vols., Parisiis, 1889-1897), I, pt. 1, nn. 452, 453 (hereafter cited *Chartularium*).

[43] Denifle-Chatelain, *Cartularium,* I, pt. 1, n. 20, n. 246. Instruction in the Latin language was to be given from *Priscianus.* The study of the ancient poets, historians and orators was ommitted at this time, as also the study of the newly recovered Metaphysics and Natural Philosophy of Aristotle. The Old and New Dialectic of Aristotle, i.e., the *Organon* and the *Isagoge* of Porphyry were included with the *Barbarismus,* i.e., Book III of the *Ars Major* of Donatus and the *Topics* of Boethius. The courses in Philosophy consisted of studies in the Ethics of Aristotle, Arithmetic, Geometry, Music and Astronomy. By 1366 another set of Statutes reveals that other works of Aristotle were added to the required courses: *Physica, De Anima, De Generatione et Conceptione, De Caelo, De Mundo, Parva Naturalia* and the *Liber Mechanicae.*

[44] "Circa statum Theologorum statuimus quod nullus Parisius legat citra 35 aetatis suae annum, et nisi studuerit per octo annos ad minus, et libros fideliter et in scholis audiverit, et quinque annis audiat Theologiam antequam privatas lectiones legat publice. . . —*Loc. cit.*

[45] Denifle-Chatelain, *Chartularium,* II, n. 1189.

for their students, and obtained even more extensive dispensations for individual members of their Orders.[46]

A student of the Arts at Paris pursued a course which was divided into two phases. In the first he was a scholar only. In the second he was permitted and required to do some teaching himself, although he continued his studies under a Master. At Paris, as at Bologna, study and teaching were blended in the university. A thesis had to be defended before an opponent or a board of opponents as a customary procedure. By 1279 it became obligatory for students of the Arts *"to determine."*[47]

D. The University of Oxford.

There is great discussion among historians about the exact origin of a *Studium Generale* at Oxford. The controversy is concerned with Oxford as an outgrowth of the monastic schools already there, or with Oxford originating as the result of an academic migration from Paris, which was then the ordinary place of higher education for English priests.[48] The documentary history of Oxford begins in 1209, when, after a pitched battle between the students and the people of the town, many students and Masters left Oxford. Some went to Reading, the nearest large town, others to the great Mother-University at Paris, and others to Cambridge and began there a *Studium Generale*. By 1214 Oxford had an ordinance from a legate of the Holy See settling the difficulty, the matter of reparations and the appointment of a Chancellor by the Bishop of Lincoln.[49]

The magisterial guilds at Oxford eventually presented one elected from among themselves to the Bishop of Lincoln for confirmation as Chancellor. He was entrusted with the general super-

---

46 *Ibidem,* nn. 992, 1002.

47 Denifle-Chatelain, *Chartularium,* I, pt. 1, n. 485. *Determinatio* was the name given to the examination undertaken by a student before he could present himself as a candidate for the Chancellor's License.

48 Cf. Rashdall, III, 5-23; Salter, *Medieval Archives of the University of Oxford* (2 vols., Oxford Historical Society, The Clarendon Press, 1917-1919), I, 65-91 (hereafter cited *Medieval Archives*).

49 Salter, *Medieval Archives,* I, 2-4; 8-9.

vision of all the schools, and he could enforce his regulations by means of banishment from Oxford, imprisonment, and even excommunication.[50]

In the schools of Oxford there were only two *Nations,* since there was only one recognized racial or national distinction, that between the English to the North of Trent and that of the English to the South of Trent, the *Boreales* and the *Australes.* The Northern and Southern Masters of Arts were presided over by their elected Proctors or Rectors.[51]

In 1254, Oxford, like its Mother-University at Paris, received the confirmation of all its *immunities, liberties and laudable, ancient and reasonable customs and good and approved constitutions* from Pope Innocent IV.[52] The distinction as to *Nations,* so vital a part of the constitutions of Paris, disappeared at Oxford by 1274, and the Faculty of Arts voted as a single body thereafter.[53]

The great constitutional peculiarity of Oxford was the almost entire absence of a separate faculty organization. At Oxford, as never at Paris, the University itself settled every detail of the curriculum and the internal discipline of all faculties. Only the University dispensed from the regulations made by the University after they had been approved by the Chancellor.[54]

The courses of study at Oxford were those given and required at Paris, i.e., the Arts and the Three Philosophies,[55] Theology,

---

[50] Anstey, *Munimenta Academica* (2 vols., The Rolls Series, London; Longmans, Green, Reader and Dyer, 1868), I, 285 ff.

[51] Anstey, *Munimenta Academica,* I, 81; Gibson, *Statuta Antiqua Universitatis Oxoniensis* (Oxford, Oxford Historical Society, 1831), pp. 64-66, 133-134 (hereafter cited *Statuta Antiqua*).

[52] Anstey, *Munimenta Academica,* I, 26-30.

[53] The articles of peace drawn up after one of the faction disagreements between *North* and *South* in 1274 makes this clear: "Proviso insuper quod de cetero partes non fiant seu nominentur in universitate, sed unum sit collegium et unum corpus; aliis nihilominus obligationibus penalibus per universitatem prius ordinatus in suo robore duraturis."—Salter, *Medieval Archives,* I, 27, 28; Anstey, *Munimenta Academica,* I, 92.

[54] Gibson, *Statuta Antiqua,* p. 18.

[55] The Natural, Moral and Metaphysical Philosophy of Aristotle was part of the Arts' Course. Anstey, *Munimenta Academica,* I, 285; Gibson, *Statuta Antiqua,* pp. 234, 235.

Medicine, Civil Law, Canon Law, Music, Mathematics and Astronomy had their own faculties and granted degrees. There was more emphasis on Mathematics and Astronomy at Oxford than at Paris.

E. Colleges.

The College is another and a significant contribution of the medieval university to modern education. University Colleges, which became so numerous at Paris and Oxford, were originally the *hospicia,* i.e., the hostels, halls or boarding places of the students.[56] The need of domestic supervision over such numbers of young men was obvious to the students themselves. Being democratic in government, the students elected their own principal or regent, who was responsible for the rent, board and other expenses. Pious benefactors frequently founded or endowed these *hospicia* for poor students, as, for instance, the modest endowment of beds in the Hotel Dieu at Paris, known as the *Collège des Dix-Huit,* for the support of eighteen poor scholars.[57] The convents of religious Orders were designated as university colleges. The students from the beginning attended the lectures of the university.

The Latin conquest of Constantinople in 1204 provided, at Paris, for the first establishment of a college which was for young men already past the grammar-school age. In 1205 Pope Innocent III issued a Bull,[58] inviting young Parisian ecclesiastics to leave Paris for study in the East, while Greek youths were to be sent to Paris to study in the School of Theology. This College of Constantinople was to be a means which would help the Pope in his work of reunifying the Church. The Orders began to establish colleges for their own men in Paris. The English Abbot of Clairvaux, Stephen of Lexington (1243-1257), in 1246 initiated such a col-

---

[56] Denifle-Chatelain, *Chartularium,* II, n. 1007.

[57] Denifle-Chatelain, *Chartularium,* II, Intro., n. 50: "Tali facta conditione quod ejusdem domus procuratores decem et octo scholaribus clericis lectos sufficientes et singulis mensibus duodecim annos de confraria quae colligitur in archa, perpetuo administrabunt."

[58] Denifle-Chatelain, *Chartularium,* I, pt. 1, n. 3.

lege for the men of his own Cistercian Abbey who were to study Theology in Paris, after he had received the approval of Pope Innocent IV.[59]

In 1257 the most famous of the Colleges of Paris was founded by Robert de Sorbonne (1201-1274), Canon of Cambray, and afterwards of Paris. Here the original plan called for an establishment for sixteen students of Theology, four from each Nation, i.e., French, Norman, Picard and English, represented at the University. King St. Louis IX gave part of the site, and collections were taken up in churches to finance the project. The supreme government of the foundation and the control of the burses were entrusted to a Board of Governors, namely, the Archdeacon and Chancellor of Paris, the Doctors of Theology and the Rector and the Proctors of the University.[60]

Gradually, instruction of a lower and higher grade was given in the colleges. Gradually, too, the Universities obtained control of the colleges and supervised the private life of the students. With this control there also resulted a more generous provision for the support of poor scholars. In Paris alone over sixty-seven colleges were founded before the year 1500. The French Revolution brought about the disappearance of the whole collegiate system in Paris, but at Oxford and Cambridge the early colleges, v.g., Balliol College and Merton Hall, reproduced many features of the Parisian organization.[61]

It was from the two centers, Bologna, the *Student University*, and Paris, the *Master University*, that other universities grew. Thus Oxford (1167) and Cambridge (1209) were outgrowths of Paris; Vicenza (1204), Arezzo (1215) and Padua (1222); of Bologna. The university movement spread to Spain, and three universities were opened there in the XIII century: Palencia, Salamanca and Vallodolid. The University of Lisbon was also founded in the same century. The University of Toulouse, established by Pope Gregory IX in 1233, and the University of Naples,

---

[59] *Ibidem*, n. 133.

[60] *Ibidem*, nn. 302, 448, 515, 519.

[61] Rashdall, I, 533.

set up by Emperor Frederick II in 1244, afford an example of the most significant kind of foundation for the whole university movement. They were created by papal and imperial decrees respectively. All subsequent universities received their charters from one or both of these sources, the majority from the former.

During the Middle Ages, before the Reformation, eighty-one universities were established throughout all of Europe. Germany, Belgium, Bohemia, Poland, Hungary, Denmark, Sweden and Scotland all had universities. Kings, noblemen and bishops were the organizers of many universities, but the charter came from a higher and more widely recognized authority. The papal recognition was most coveted, for the Church, established throughout the world and enjoying universal jurisdiction, was held competent above all other powers to authorize great teaching institutions.[62]

The universities constitute the great achievement of the Middle Ages in the intellectual sphere. "Their organization and their traditions," says Rashdall, "their studies and their exercises affected the progress and intellectual development of Europe more powerfully, or, perhaps it should be said, more exclusively, than any schools in all likelihood will ever do again."[63]

Men who were eager for a preparation for living gave the lasting impetus, so it appears, for the origin and growth of universities in the Middle Ages. They sought freedom and direction for their study of truths and of things. They sought to probe into the mysteries of man's mind and to learn of the intrinsic organism of his body. They were enthusiastic about the Revelation of God and the Law of His Church. They came and found help and instruction under the careful guidance of princes and popes. They wanted education for themselves and for others, and it was theirs in the universities of the Middle Ages.

---

[62] Pace, "Universities" *The Catholic Encyclopedia* (15 vols., Index and Supplement, New York, 1907-1922), XV, 191; Ottaviani, *Institutiones Iuris Publici Ecclesiastici* (3. ed., 2 vols., Romae, Typis Polyglottis Vaticanis, 1947-1948), II, 240, 241.

[63] *The Universities of Europe in the Middle Ages,* I, 533.

Section 2. The United States of America.

The history of the foundations of Catholic institutions for higher learning is impressive. Along with the prodigious work of establishing and maintaining primary and secondary schools, bishops, priests, religious Orders and Communities and likewise the Catholic people displayed great effort, care and anxiety for the institution and development of Catholic colleges and universities.

From the foundation of Georgetown College in 1789 to the year 1850 thirty-eight institutions of higher education were founded. A brief summary of some of the first foundations which have persevered to our own day will show the hardships and opposition which confronted the pioneers of the Catholic university movement in America. The faith, desire and tenacity of purpose of the early founders is clearly manifest when it is considered that twenty-eight such foundations were functioning in 1850. Eighteen of those institutions had charters from the various states in which they were located, and seven had been raised to the rank of universities. Thirteen were under the direction of the Jesuits, and seven were under the management of diocesan authorities. The Sulpicians, Vincentians, Holy Cross Fathers, Augustinians, Benedictines, Franciscans and Brothers of Mary, all were operating their own colleges. One college at New Windsor, Maryland, was under the supervision of Catholic laymen.[64] The geographical area covered by the Catholic colleges and universities in 1850 included fifteen states and the District of Columbia.[65]

The first Catholic school for higher learning originated at Newtown in the Maryland Colony, in 1677, as a school for the teaching of the classics.[66] James A. Burns (1867-1940) held that, from

[64] Cassidy, *Catholic College Foundations and Development in the United States (1677-1850)* (Washington, D.C., 1924), pp. 72, 96 (hereafter cited Cassidy).

[65] Cassidy, *passim;* Maryland, Kentucky, New York, Massachusetts, Indiana, Michigan, Missouri, Pennsylvania, Ohio, Illinois, Louisiana, Delaware, Virginia, Alabama and Kansas.

[66] A letter sent to the Jesuit Superiors in Europe in 1681 reads: "Four years ago, a school for humanities was opened by our Society in the center of the country directed by two of the Fathers; and the native youth, applying themselves assiduously to study, made good progress. Maryland

its start as an elementary school, Newtown developed into an institute with a complete college curriculum, because of the eager desires of the Jesuits to establish such an institute in Maryland and the fact that the faculty at Newtown was increased in 1681.[67] In 1688 persecution put an end to the Newtown School in Maryland,[68] forcing the Jesuits to establish their college at Bohemia, near the borders of Pennsylvania and Delaware. In 1765 this school was closed because of the tirades of enemies and the attempt to outlaw it in the Maryland Assembly.[69]

The Revolutionary War brought the end of religious persecution in America, but with it came an education that was sectarian in character. The Very Rev. John Carroll, after his first visitation as Prefect Apostolic, saw the dangers to the Faith in such a system of education.[70] The first building was begun in 1788 for the Academy at Georgetown, which in the beginning did not receive boarders. The first teachers were to be seculars, "of which many and tolerably good ones" had requested appointments to the faculty. From such a beginning it was hoped that many of the students would be called to the service of the Church. These seminarians, then, would combine teaching in the Academy with their ecclesiastical training for ordination.[71] After Bishop Carroll's return

---

and the recently established school sent two boys to St. Omer, who yielded in abilities to few Europeans, when competing for the honor of being first in their class."—Treacy, *Old Catholic Maryland and Its Early Jesuit Missionaries* (Swedesboro, N. J., 1899), p. 95.

[67] *The Catholic School System in the United States* (New York: Benziger Bros., 1908), p. 103 (hereafter cited Burns).

[68] William III was petitioned to save the people of Maryland "from the arbitrary will and pleasure of a tyrannical Popish government under which they had so long groaned."—Shea, *History of the Catholic Church in the United States* (4 vols., Akron, Ohio, 1886-1892), I, 91.

[69] Burns, p. 116.

[70] In December of 1785 he wrote: "The object nearest my heart now, and the only one that can give consistency to our religious views in this country, is the establishment of a school and afterwards of a seminary for young clergymen."—Shea, *History of Georgetown College* (New York: P. F. Collier, 1891), p. 9.

[71] Guilday, *The Life and Times of John Carroll* (New York: The Encyclopedia Press, 1922), p. 457.

from a trip to England to solicit funds, the Academy at Georgetown received its first students in 1791, and in subsequent years the college grew in numbers and prestige. An act of Congress in May of 1815 raised it to the rank of a university.

Another great impetus for American, Catholic, college and university education was occasioned by the destructive Revolution in France. The suppression of churches and schools in France turned the attention of the Superior-General of the Society of St. Sulpice towards America. His first thought had been for a house of Sulpicians in the Mississippi Valley. The Papal Nuncio at Paris suggested that he speak with Bishop Carroll, then in England, about a seminary for the Diocese of Baltimore. In July of 1791 a group of Sulpicians arrived in America, and by the fall of that year they were ready to receive the first five students who were prepared to begin their studies for the Holy Priesthood. In 1791 the ambition of Bishop Carroll seemed ultimately realized.[72] In a few years, inasmuch as no ecclesiastical students were forthcoming from Georgetown, the Sulpicians resolved, with the approval of Bishop Carroll, to open an academy. In 1799, in a new building, St. Mary's College began to receive students. In 1803 students from many parts of America, without distinction of creed, were attending St. Mary's. In 1805 the Maryland Legislature raised St. Mary's to the rank of a university and granted it permission to confer degrees in the arts, the sciences and the liberal professions.

After an agreement with the Jesuits that Loyola University in Baltimore should be opened in the year of 1852, St. Mary's College became a thing of the past. The Sulpicians found that their attention and energies were required for the work of preparing candidates for the Holy Priesthood.[73]

The remote, western part of America was to have the benefit of two Catholic colleges before 1825. Bishop Doubourg, long associated with the education of young men,[74] was consecrated as

[72] *Memorial Volume of the Centenary of St. Mary's Seminary of St. Sulpice* (Baltimore, Md., 1891), p. 7 (hereafter cited *Memorial Volume*).

[73] *Memorial Volume,* p. 8.

[74] He was President of Georgetown College from 1796 to 1799.—*Memorial Volume,* p. 7.

Bishop of Lousiana in 1815. In 1817 he secured the co-operation of the Vincentians to carry out his plan for establishing a seminary and a college in St. Louis.[75] The college opened in December of 1814, and the teaching of the ancient classics continued there under the diocesan clergy after the Vincentian, Father de Andreis (1778-1820), its first President, had died. In 1826, however, the college was forced to close because of the burdens of pastoral duties which had to be assumed by the members of the faculty.[76]

A new college was begun in 1828. It was entrusted to the care of the Jesuits by Bishop Rosati. In its first year it had one hundred and fifty pupils in attendance, and in 1833 it was incorporated by a special act of the State Legislature as "The St. Louis University." In 1842 a Medical School was added, and a Law Department in 1843.[77]

The Catholic colleges for women were for the most part, outgrowths of the early academies. In 1895, the Academy of Notre Dame in Baltimore petitioned the Maryland Legislature for a charter which would permit it to grant degrees. In 1899 the first degrees were granted by this new "Collegiate Institue." The Academy of St. Elizabeth, founded in 1859 by the Sisters of Charity of Mother Seton, sought and was granted a college charter by the State of New Jersey. In June of 1903 St. Elizabeth's College granted its first degrees at Convent Station. Trinity College in Washington, D. C., began as a college, and in 1904 the first class was graduated with degrees.[78]

These, in summary, evince the humble and difficult origins of Catholic college and university education in the United States. The faith, sacrifice and zeal of the bishops, priests, religious and

---

[75] Clarke, *Lives of the Deceased Bishops of the Catholic Church in the United States* (2 vols., New York, 1872), I, 229.

[76] Hill, *Historical Sketches of the St. Louis University* (St. Louis: Patrick Fox, 1879), p. 5.

[77] Cassidy, pp. 40, 41.

[78] Mother Grace Damman, "The American Catholic College for Women," *Essays on Catholic Education* (Wash. D.C., C.U.A. Press, 1942), pp. 178, 179.

faithful have raised the number of colleges and universities to 247.[79]

Article 2. Positive Legislation—The Middle Ages to the Present.

It has been noted that universities and colleges were, at first, loose confederations of students or teachers. The subsequent formation of corporations for the twofold purpose of protection and improvement, as also the expansion and multiplication of these organizations and the difficulties incident to their operation, called for a gradual enactment of legislation. It was to come, little by little, from the popes and the civil rulers. Their plans gave impetus and solidarity to the entire movement in the Middle Ages when they founded and erected new universities,[80] and approved and endowed with privileges those already in existence.[81]

The earlier pieces of legislation touching universities had reference to the *licentia docendi* and the support of clerics who pursued higher studies. For those who had successfully completed their courses, the papal legislation provided that they were to be granted the *licentia docendi,* free of any tax or charges.[82] When Pope Alexander II (1159-1181) discovered that the custom of

---

[79] *The Official Catholic Directory,* (New York), P. J. Kennedy & Sons, 1955), chart, p. 1132.

[80] The University of Toulouse was constituted by Pope Gregory IX in 1233. Ottaviani (*Institutiones Iuris Publici Ecclesiastici,* II, 241) lists fourteen universities erected through papal documents. Frederick II, in 1224, founded the University of Naples. Cf. Denifle, pp. 452, ff.

[81] Thus the University of Salamanca, which had been founded by the civil power, was given papal approbation by Alexander IV in 1255. The endowment of Chairs and Lectures was another means used by the popes to advance the cause of the universities. Cf. Wernz, *Ius Decretalium,* III, pt. 1., n. 85.

[82] . . . Pro licentia vero docendi nullus pretium exigat, vel sub obtentu alicuius consuetudinis ab eis qui docent, aliquid quaerat; nec docere quemquam, qui sit idoneus, petita licentia, interdicat. Cf. *Decretales D. Gregorii Papae IX, una cum glossis* (Romae, 1582), c. 1, *de magistris et ne aliquid exigatur pro licentia docendi,* V, 5.

exacting a fee for the granting of the *licentia docendi* persisted in some parts of France, he ordered the custom abolished under pain of severe penalty.[83]

Those clerics who desired to make the studies necessary for degrees which would qualify them for positions as teachers were to be given material support for their needs throughout the five years they spent as students, in the legislation of Pope Honorius III (1216-1227).[84]

When a period of seven years became necessary for encompassing the courses required for a Doctorate, Boniface VIII (1294-1303) granted to bishops the faculty of dispensing clerics from the law of residence for those years and insisted again on material support for such students.[85]

The intellectual and moral upheaval of the Reformation sought

---

[83] . . . Mandamus, quatenus (consuetudine ipsa de vestris ecclesiis exstirpata) sub anathematis interminatione hoc inhibere curetis, districte percipientes ut quicumque viri idonei et litterati voluerint regere studia litterarum, sine molestia et exactione qualibet scholas regere permittantur. Si quis vero huiusmodi prohibitionis vel praecepti extiterint transgressores, eos officiis et dignitatibus spolietis.—C. 3, X, *de magistris et ne aliquid exigatur pro licentia docendi*, V, 5.

[84] Volumus et mandamus ut statutum, in concilio generali de magistris theologis per singulas metropoles statuendis, inviolabiliter observetur, statuentes ut, quia super hoc propter raritatem magistrorum se possent aliqui forsitan excusare, ab ecclesiarum praelatis et capitulis ad theologicae professionis studium aliqui docibiles destinentur . . . qui ad iustitiam valeant plurimos erudire, quibus si proprii ecclesiastici non sufficiunt, praedicti necessaria subministrent. Docentes vero in theologica facultate, dum in scholis docuerint, et studentes in ipsa, integre per annos quinque percipiant de licentia Sedis Apostolicae proventus praebendarum et beneficiorum suorum, non obstante aliqua alia consuetudine, vel statuto, dum denario fraudari non debeant, in vinea Domini operantes.—C. 5, X, *de magistris etc.*, V, 5.

[85] Nos super hoc multorum instantia excitati frequenter, volentes cupientibus in scientia proficere, ut fructum in Dei ecclesia suo tempore offere valeant opportunum, utiliter providere, praesenti consitutione sancimus, ut episcopi . . . dispensare possint libere . . . —*Liber Sextus Decretalium D. Bonifacii Papae VIII, suae integritati cum Clementinis et Extravagantibus, earumque Glossis restitutis* (Romae, 1582), c. 34. *de electione et electi potestate,* I, 6, in VI°.

to strip the Church of all authority. In Germany and England, civil authority replaced the Church in the field of higher education. The Council of Trent (1545-1563), recognizing that a true reformation must be linked with education on all levels, followed the lead of the Commission of Reform appointed by Pope Paul III in 1538. That Commission numbered among its members Cardinal Pole, who in February of 1556 made clear in his legislation for England that the education of young men was to be intensified, even though some of them would not be candidates for Holy Orders.[86] That the Council was in accord with the findings in the report of the Pope's Commission is clear from its legislation that lectureships in Holy Scripture and the Liberal Arts be established and supported by local ordinaries.[87] Here, then, was provision for higher study under the supervision of the Church, even in those areas where its teaching was excluded from universities and colleges. The unity between nations had been destroyed by the Reformation, and education suffered from the subsequent

---

86 J. Hardouin, *Acta Conciliorum et Epistolae Decretales ac Constitutiones Summorum Pontificum* (12 vols., Parisiis, 1715), X, 409.

87 "The same holy council, adhering to the pious decisions of the sovereign pontiffs and of approved councils, and accepting and adding to them, that the heavenly treasure of the sacred books which the Holy Ghost has with the greatest liberality delivered to many may not lie neglected, has ordained and decreed that in those churches in which there exists a prebend or a benefice with an obligation attached, or other income by whatever name it may be known, set aside for instructors in sacred theology, the bishops, archbishops, primates, and other ecclesiastical superiors of those localities compel, even by a reduction of their revenues, those who hold such prebend, benefice or income, to expound and interpret the Holy Scriptures, either personally if they are competent, otherwise by a competent substitute to be chosen by the bishops, archbishops, primates, or other superiors of those places. . . . In metropolitan and cathedral churches . . . let the metropolitan or the bishop . . . provide in such a way with the advice of the chapter that the instructions in Holy Scripture may be procured; so, however, that all other instructions, whether established by custom or any other agency, be by no means on that account omitted."—Sess. V, *de ref.*, c. 1: The preceding translation is that of H. J. Schroeder, *Canons and Decrees of The Council of Trent, Original Text with English Translation* (St. Louis, B. Herder Book Co., 1941), pp. 24, 25 (hereafter cited Schroeder).

growth of nationalism and factions. The Council of Trent gave the direction for higher education, which was thenceforth to proceed along diocesan lines or to look to such directives as derived from the papal constitution and erection of the university.[88]

The Providence of God intervened for Catholic higher education in the XVI century in yet another way. Newly founded religious Orders, dedicated by their Constitutions to education, flourished despite the violent opposition of heretics. Foremost among them, the Jesuits had as specific objects in their approved Constitutions the instruction of youth in schools and colleges, and the lecturing on philosophy and theology in the universities.[89] Their labors were most instrumental in the founding and expanding of new colleges and universities at the invitation of many bishops.[90]

The expansion and growth of higher education in America were fostered and approved by popes and councils. Pope Pius IX (1846-1878) was most insistent that universities and colleges be

---

[88] Sess. XXV, *de ref., c.* 2: ". . . all those to whom pertains the care, visitation, and reform of universities and of [houses of] general studies, shall diligently see to it that the canons and decrees of this holy council are integrally received by the universities and that the masters, doctors, and others in those universities teach and interpret the things that are of Catholic faith in conformity therewith, and at the beginning of each year bind themselves by solemn oath to the observance of this ordinance; and if there be any other matters in the aforesaid universities that need correction and reform, they shall for the advancement of religion and ecclesiastical discipline be reformed and put in order by those to whom it pertains. Those universities, however, that are immediately subject to the protection and visitation of the supreme Roman pontiff, His Holiness will provide for in the matters of visitation and reform through his delegates in the manner aforesaid and as shall seem to him most beneficial." —Schroeder, p. 234.

[89] T. Hughes, Loyola and the Educational System of the Jesuits (New York, Chas. Scribner's Sons, 1892), pp. 53 ff.

[90] R. Schwickerath (*Jesuit Education: Its History and Principles in Light of Modern Educational Problems* [St. Louis, B. Herder Book Co., 1904], pp. 142-145) pointed to a University which opened in Cologne in 1558 with 800 students, and to one in Utrecht with 1000. The total number of students in more than 700 universities and colleges was estimated at 210,000 by 1773.

built and supported in Canada and the United States.[91] The III Plenary Council of Baltimore (1884) strongly recommended that as many Catholic colleges and universities be founded as were required, and that they were to be fully equipped to meet the needs of students and the demands of the time.[92] Pope Leo XIII (1878-1903) continued to urge the establishment of new Catholic colleges and universities,[93] and gave pontifical approbation to the Catholic University of America in 1889.[94]

The grave concern in our own day for the establishment of higher schools of education is clearly manifested in the Code and in the official papal pronouncements. The Code first speaks of the duty of providing for the Christian education of all the faithful from the time of their childhood,[95] and reminds parents and those who take their place of the serious obligation in this matter.[96] The Church claims for itself the right to establish colleges and universities,[97] and desires that such be established and supported through the co-operation of the faitful.[98]

Pope Pius XI's encyclical letter, *Divini illius Magistri,* of December 31, 1929, requires the establishment of schools which are truly Catholic,[99] and of schools which are to be staffed with good, zealous, unselfish teachers.[100] His Apostolic Constitution, *Deus Scientiarum Dominus,* of May 24, 1931,[101] recites the brilliant achievements of the Church in the founding and the fostering of

---

[91] *Acta Sanctae Sedis* (41 vols., Romae, 1865-1908), IX (1875-1876), 369 ff.

[92] *Acta et Decreta Concilii Plenarii Baltimorensis Tertii* (Baltimorae: John Murphy, 1886), n. 209 (hereafter cited *Acta et Decreta*).

[93] *Acta Sanctae Sedis,* XXI (1888-1889), 513; XXII (1889-1890), 201.

[94] Litt. Apost., *Magni nobis gaudii,* 7 mart. 1889—*Leonis XIII, Pontificis Maximi Acta* (23 vols., Romae, Typographia Vaticana, 1881-1905), IX, 69-72.

[95] Canons 1113 and 1372, § 1.

[96] Can. 1372, § 2.

[97] Canons 1375 and 1376.

[98] Can. 1379, § 2, § 3.

[99] *Acta Apostolicae Sedis, Commentarium Officiale* (Romae, 1909-), XXII (1930), 77, 78 (hereafter cited *AAS*).

[100] *Ibidem,* pp. 80, 81.

[101] *AAS,* XXIII (1931), 241-262.

universities, and proposes a continuous expansion to combat the one thing the Church fears, the *ignorantia veritatis*.[102]

Pope Pius XII, in a Radio Address to the Inter-American Congress on Catholic Education on October 14, 1948,[103] reminded the delegates of the need of universities and of centers of advanced studies in which religious instruction will be given its rightful place of honor. In a letter to Cardinal Van Roey, Archbishop of Malines, Belgium,[104] the Holy Father encouraged the Congress of Education in its renewed study of the *veritable Charter of Christian Education,* given by Pope Pius XI in his encyclical letter, *Divini illius Magistri,* in their present struggle with the civil authorities over Catholic education.

---

[102] *Ibidem,* p. 245.

[103] *AAS,* XL (1948), 465-468.

[104] *L'Osservatore Romano,* September 5-6, 1955.

CHAPTER II

THE REFORMATION AND THE GROWTH OF NON-CATHOLIC UNIVERSITIES AND COLLEGES.

Article 1. The Growth in Europe.

The XVI century, one of turbulence and confusion, brought many lasting changes to the world. The peoples of Europe were harrassed with political, economic and religious differences. Luther, Calvin, Henry VIII and others, aided by the corruption and scandal then prevalent in the Church, had embarked on their courses of rebellion. The Reformation, a sudden revolt against the Church and ecclesiastical authority, struck a severe blow at the educational institutions then in existence with the result that schools were disorganized and in many places closed. A Protestant historian says of the Reformation in Germany:

> The first effect of these events on the educational institutions was destructive; the old schools and universities were so bound up with the Church in all respects—socially, legally and economically—that they could not but be involved in its downfall. The mere cessation of the prospects of clerical livings was bound to exercise a deterrent influence in regard to school and university studies. Then followed the Peasants' War, with its unmerciful devastation on both sides; and thus it came about that the ten years between 1525 and 1535 resulted in a depression of learning and education which is without parallel in history. The figures of attendance at the universities were reduced to one-quarter of their former amount, and the same was probably the case with the schools, so that Erasmus could exclaim: "Wherever Luther prevails, the cause of literature and learning is lost."[1]

[1] F. Paulsen, *German Education, Past and Present* (Tr. by T. Lorenz, New York: Chas. Scribner's Sons, 1908), p. 54 (hereafter cited *German Education*).

A divided Germany, divided by reason of governments and faiths, began the work of restoring its universities after the havoc of the Reformation. Each government sought to provide a university within its own domain which would give the instruction necessary to provide leaders. A university was desired that it might impart religious instruction in harmony with the tenets of the particular government; that it might provide training for secular leaders under the watchful eye of the government and, finally, that it might make unnecessary the expensive attendance of students in a foreign university. In this method the old ideal of the *studium generale* was destroyed. There was no longer the international freedom of transfer to different schools or of an exchange of ideas. There were positive prohibitions against attendance at a university other than the one existing in a given territorial division. The divisions and prohibitions in Protestant territories increased with the passage of time. Thus, even in the XVII and XVIII centuries, the people of Brandenburg were repeatedly forbidden to attend the Saxon university at Wittenberg, home of the old Lutheran orthodoxy, because the Saxons had gone over to the Reformed faith. The fear of heresy made for a determined effort to control instruction in greater measure than at any time before. Those states which professed Lutheranism were much more anxious about university instruction and the strict supervision over it than even the Catholic states, since apostasy from Lutheranism, still undeveloped in its theological terms and teaching, was possible in two directions, that of Calvinism or that of Catholicism.[2]

Philip Melanchthon (1497-1560) wielded great influence in Germany as a teacher, scholar and educational organizer. By the time he had reached the age of twenty-one, he was received into the University of Wittenberg as a professor of Greek. It was there that he first came into close relationship with Luther and was won over by him to the study of theology. From Wittenberg, after he had become the great exponent of the evangelical doctrine and the founder of Protestant theology, he furnished schoolmasters and

[2] F. Paulsen, *The German Universities and University Study* (Tr. by F. Thilly, New York: Chas. Scribner's Sons, 1906), pp. 35-37 (hereafter cited *German Universities*).

advised local authorities on questions connected with schools. His textbooks had an important influence in Protestant Germany. The *Loci Communes* was the textbook in evangelical theology. Manuals and guides for various school subjects, and especially his Latin and Greek grammars, furthered humanism in Protestant schools.[3]

The theological faculties at the German universities were the most important in the early period of restoration. In the XVIII century, however, the adoption of the modern philosophy of Christian Wolff, (1679-1754) who taught at Halle from 1707 to 1725 and again from 1740 to 1754, began to make inroads into the place of primary importance of the faculties of theology. He taught that philosophy was to be unhampered in its search for truth. It was to be free from all theological assumptions in its theory. In practice, philosophy was not to have a theological basis. In his *Vernünftige Gedanken,* he maintained that law and morals must be based upon a rational knowledge of human life and society.[4]

It was this philosophy which prevailed at all Protestant universities. The next development, that of academic freedom, was not long in coming from a system in which reason alone was acknowledged as the guide for all thought and all practice. In the XIX century, territorial barriers and those of the various churches were put aside, and the most frequent phrase in university thinking and planning was "free scientific research." The University of Berlin (1809) was the embodiment of the new spirit. In the words of Paulsen (1846-1908):

> It may be safely asserted that the new University of Berlin was expressly organized in direct contrast to the higher schools of the military dictator. Its principle was to be, not unity and subordination, but freedom and independence. The professors were not to be teaching and examining state-officials, but independent scholars. Instruction was to be carried on not according to a prescribed order, but with a view to liberty of teaching and learning. The aim was not encyclo-

---

[3] K. Hartfelder, *Philip Menlanchthon, Praeceptor Germaniae* (Berlin: A. Hoffman, 1899), p. 34.

[4] *German Universities,* p. 45.

> pedic infomation, but genuine scientific culture. The students were not to be regarded as merely preparing for future service as state officials, but as young men to be trained in independence of thought and in intellectual and moral freedom by means of an untrammelled study of science.[5]

In England the effect of the Reformation of the Church was much the same as in Germany with respect to universities and colleges. The names were different, i.e., Henry VIII (1509-1547) and Edward VI (1547-1553), but the process was the same. Within ten years by Certificates, Warrants and Commissions of Enquiry,[6] Henry VIII had suppressed 600 monasteries and 90 colleges.[7] Before Henry VIII's program of educational reform was finished, almost 300 schools which had been built in and around Oxford were dissolved, and their revenues appropriated for the building of a new navy and for distribution among his favorites and supporters.[8] Under his son, Edward VI, there was no lessening of the effects of the royal confiscations.[9]

The religious struggle in England was to bring forth a third religious group in the land, namely those who sought a complete break from the Catholic and Anglican positions. The Puritans, after the time of Elizabeth (1558-1603), made their way into the system of education which sought through courses in dialectic, mathematics, rhetoric, philosophy and theology, to prepare students for forceful discussion and argumentation in support of the State and the Church. It was the State, however, that was in charge of education, although the management of the schools remained in the hands of the Protestant clergy. Liberty of conscience had been the point of greatest insistence in the early days

---

[5] *German Universities*, p. 52.

[6] A. F. Leach, *English Schools at the Reformation* (Westminster, A. Constable & Co., 1896), pt. II, i-v (hereafter cited Leach).

[7] F. P. Graves, *A History of Education During the Middle Ages* (New York: The Macmillan Co., 1910), p. 195 (hereafter cited Graves, *History*).

[8] E. Magevney, *The Reformation and Education* (New York: The Cathedral Library Association, 1903), p. 34.

[9] Leach, p. 5.

of the leaders of the revolt. It was that same liberty which was denied to others who were in disagreement, and the various Protestant sects were completely intolerant of any opposing doctrine, even despite their basic tenet for the right to private interpretation. It was the purpose of education to prepare men to become intelligent enough for this private interpretation and, in that sense, it was religious education. Authority in the form of obedient acceptance of dogma was to yield to the application of reason to the Scriptures. Men were to be trained to affiliate with the Protestant churches, but education was also to be as much for the sake of the State as of the church.[10]

The path to Realism, Naturalism and Rationalism was pointed out by Francis Bacon (1561-1626) and John Locke (1632-1704) in their educational theories. Rabelais (1495-1533), Montaigne (1533-1592) and Mulcaster (1530-1611), among others, had already become vocal in their lack of respect for the humanistic, formal education of their day. Bacon's fundamental thesis in education was that knowledge is power, and that if men knew better they would do better. He held that the new social order could and would spring into being through the scientific investigation of natural phenomena by means of inductive reasoning. The place and function of education was to be realized by the dissemination of scientific knowledge through schools. He did did not reject divine revelation, but it was to have no part in education, because all living was to be based on scientific knowledge.[11]

Locke's aim in education was threefold: (1) vigor of body; (2) virtue of the soul with its manifestation in good breeding and wisdom in conduct, and (3) knowledge or mental acquirements. This latter aim was to be subordinated to the others. He was most careful to insist, as a former tutor, that the children of nobles were to be reared physically and morally with great care, "that most to be taken care of is the gentleman's calling. For if those of that rank are by their education once set right, they will quickly bring all

---

[10] Graves, *History,* pp. 196-205.

[11] W. Kane, *An Essay toward a History of Education* (Chicago: Loyola Univ. Press, 1935), pp. 321-325.

the rest into order."[12] In his empiric philosophy of the *tabula rasa,* Locke wanted the child instructed in religion; "that he might have a true notion of God as the independent supreme Being, Author and Maker of all things, from Whom we receive all our good, and Who loves us and gives us all things: and, consequent to this, a love and reverence of this Supreme Being."[13] Although Locke held to a belief in a divine revelation, he left it open to the questioning of mere human reason.[14]

Article 2. The Growth in the United States of America.

The venture which directed the Massachusetts Colony to New England brought with it men who had been educated in England. Unlike the Virginia Colony, their aim was, primarily, religious rather than commercial. The great influence and moving spirit was in the person of John Winthrop, the first governor of the Massachusetts Colony (1629-1649). He believed that the colony would first of all be of great service to the Church in carrying the Gospel to this part of the world, while "raising a bulwark against the Kingdom of Antichrist which the Jesuits labor to rear up in those parts." Secondly, it was honorable and worthy for a Christian "to help raise and support a particular church while it is in its infancy, and to join his forces with such a company of faithful people as by a timely assistance may grow strong and prosper; and for want of it may be put to great hazard, if not wholly ruined." Thirdly, those who gave up ease and comfort and endured the hardships of the New World did by their example "give more life to the faith of God's people in their prayers for the plantation" and did "encourage others to join the more willingly in it."[15]

In 1636, the General Court of the Colony of Massachusetts Bay voted to "give 400 pounds toward a school or college." In the fol-

---

12 Dedicatory Epistle in *Thoughts Concerning Education* (Ed. by R. H. Quick, London: Cambridge Univ. Press, C. J. Clay & Sons, 1892).

13 *Ibidem,* Sect. 136.

14 *An Essay Concerning Human Understanding* (London: J. F. Dove, 1828), Book IV, Ch. 18.

15 R. C. Winthrop, *Life and Letters of John Winthrop* (2 vols., Boston: Ticknor and Fields, 1846-1847), I, 309, 310.

lowing year twelve of the most eminent men of the colony were appointed by the Court to become its governors. Six were officers of the Commonwealth and six were neighboring clergymen.[16] The college was located at Cambridge, and in 1639 it was to receive its name from John Harvard (1607-1638), who left his library of 300 volumes and half of his other property to the new college.

The method af academic government was fixed in the year 1650, when Harvard was granted a charter making it a Corporation with a Board of Overseers. The Corporation consisted of a president, five fellows and a treasurer. The Overseers had in their number six of the pastors from neighboring towns. The Overseers were to exercise the power of revision over the acts of the Corporation. Thus the control of the new college was put outside the power of the Faculty.[17]

By the year 1655, four years was the required period of attendance for a degree. The course of study, by reason of the time given to a particular subject, was divided into Philosophy, Greek, Rhetoric, Oriental Languages, Mathematics, Catechism, History and Botany. The study of Philosophy, which occupied the greatest portion of the student's time, embraced physics, logic, ethics and politics. The study of Greek was linked to the study of the New Testament. In the course in Mathematics, the students were instructed in arithmetic, geometry and astronomy.[18] There was no distinct place for Theology in the *Cambridge* of the New World as there was in the Cambridge of England. It seems, then, that the founders and governors had become so domestic that they were to be no more bound by Geneva, through Calvin and his *Institutes,* than they permitted themselves to be bound by the ecclesiastical rulings of Canterbury and York.

In 1647 the General Court passed a law requiring that all towns numbering 50 householders should provide means for the teaching

---

[16] J. Quincy, *A History of Harvard University* (2 vols., Cambridge, Mass.: J. Owen, 1840), I, 7.

[17] C. F. Thwing, *A History of Higher Education in America* (New York: D. Appleton & Co., 1906), pp. 12, 13 (hereafter cited Thwing).

[18] *Proceedings of the Massachusetts Historical Society* (Boston: The Historical Society, 1859-19—), Series 1, Vol. XIV, 211.

of reading and writing, and every town of 100 families should establish a Grammar School, which should prepare students for the college. In large towns, then, secondary education became free and obligatory by order of the civil rather than the religious power in Massachusetts. The model for these Grammar Schools was to be the Boston Latin School, which had existed from 1635.[19] In this way Harvard was assured of a steady flow of students in the years to come.

This was the pattern, then, until the successful prosecution of the Revolutionary War. Colleges to provide clergymen and public servants were to be founded from the initial impetus of private citizens and churches and through the protection and support of the civil government. Eight such colleges were founded before the War, besides Harvard.[20] The College in Pennsylvania, proposed and eventually instituted almost entirely through the efforts of Benjamin Franklin (1706-1790), was constituted for the "cultivation and improvement of a new country, wisdom, riches and strength, virtue, piety, welfare and happiness of the people." There was no mention in its Constitution of either religion or the church or the ministry.[21]

After the War of Independence, the spirit which motivated the founding of colleges took on new aspects. The National Government began to entertain two prospects with regard to higher education. First, it sought to establish a National University, a plan which actually has never been realized. Secondly, it sought to help individual states to found and promote higher education by granting aid to the individual states. The aid was to be in the form of land-grants, and on July 13, 1787, Congress passed an ordinance for the territory northwest of the Ohio River.[22] This territory

---

19 P. Brooks, *The Oldest School in America* (Boston and New York: Houghton, Mifflin & Co., 1885), p. 15.

20 William and Mary (1693), Yale (1701), Princeton (1746), Pennsylvania (1749), Columbia (1751), Brown (1762), Dartmouth (1769) and Rutgers (1770).

21 T. H. Montgomery, *A History of the University of Pennsylvania, 1749-1770* (Philadelphia: G. W. Jacobs and Co., 1900), pp. 239, 240.

22 H. S. Commager, *Documents of American History* (5. ed., New York: Appleton, Century, Crofts, Inc., 1940), pp. 129-132.

comprised the present states of Ohio, Indiana, Illinois, Michigan and Wisconsin. There were guarantees for freedom of religion, right to trial by jury, proportional representation and the obligations of contracts. There was also the enactment "that religion, morals and knowledge, being necessary to good government and the happiness of mankind, schools and the means of education shall forever be encouraged." It was affirmed in the ordinance that land, up to the size of two complete townships, was to be given for a university.[23]

Ohio, in the Northwest Territory, was the first to receive the benefits of the Ordinance of 1787. In 1802 the legislators established a university at Athens, with a land-grant of two townships. A Board of Trustees was to be appointed and they, along with the president, vice-president and teachers, were to formulate the courses of study. Future appointments to the Board of Trustees were to be made by the Legislature. This institution, then, was not a private college, but rather one which had a direct relation to the State, with no close relation to a particular church group.[24]

There was yet another significant trend accompanying the process which developed higher education in America. The influence of French educational policies and practices affected Thomas Jefferson (1743-1826) as it had moved Benjamin Franklin (1706-1790) and John Adams (1735-1826) and other Americans interested in college and university education. The desire to spread French ideas and culture in America resulted in the establishment of the Academy of Arts and Sciences in Massachusetts in 1778[25] and the beginnings of an International Institute in Virginia in 1786, which was to have affiliates in America, France, England and Belgium. The Institute was to employ experts from Europe, particularly from Paris, as teachers and leaders in scientific investigations.[26] That the Institute never actually served as a meet-

[23] *Ibidem,* Article 3, p. 131.

[24] Thwing, pp. 190, 191.

[25] *The Writings of John Adams* (7 vols., ed. by W. C. Ford, New York: The Macmillan Co., 1913-1917), IV, 259, 260.

[26] H. B. Adams, *Thomas Jefferson and the University of Virginia* (Washington, D. C.: Government Printing Office, 1888), pp. 74-77 (hereafter cited *T. Jefferson*).

ing place for French scholars, because of a lack of financial support here and abroad, was no deterrent to Jefferson's ambition to found a university which was absolutely free from sectarian, religious influence. He sought an institution for higher education which would be open to all and would be under the control of the State. The influence of the personal and the civil were united to the exclusion of the influence of any church in the University of Virginia, established in 1825.[27] The purposes of higher education as outlined by Jefferson[28] were to proceed along strictly democratic lines with a maximum of liberty and freedom for the student. The University of Virginia followed the elective system with respect to the courses for students. These were no hasty plans on the part of Jefferson. In 1789, as Governor of Virginia and a Visitor to the College of William and Mary, he had abolished the chair of Divinity and Oriental Languages and had established a chair of Law and Politics, Anatomy and Medicine and Modern Languages. It was, doubtless, the freedom of his own religious thought that led Jefferson to write of his proposed University of Virginia as a place of true academic freedom.[29]

---

[27] *Loc. cit.*

[28] 1) To form the statesmen, legislators, and judges, on whom public prosperity and individual happiness are so much to depend;

2) To expound the principles and structure of government, the laws which regulate the intercourse of nations, those formed municipally for our own government, and a sound spirit of legislation, which, banishing all unnecessary restraint on individual action, shall leave us free to do whatever does not violate the equal rights of another;

3) To harmonize and promote the interests of agriculture, manufactures, and commerce, and by well-informed views of political economy to give a free scope to the public industry;

4) To develop the reasoning faculties of our youth, enlarge their minds, cultivate their morals, and instill into them the precepts of virtue and order;

5) To enlighten them with mathematical and physical sciences, which advance the arts, and administer to the health, the subsistence, and comforts of human life; and

6) Generally to form them to habits of reflection and correct action, rendering them examples of virtue to others, and of happiness within themselves.—Adams, *T. Jefferson,* p. 89.

[29] *Ibidem,* pp. 123, 124.

The education of women, begun in academies with the addition of the contents of the Bible and the catechism to the three elementary subjects, became higher education in Oberlin Institute in Ohio in 1837. At the commencement of 1841, three women along with a number of men received degrees in Arts. Iowa (1856), Kansas and Minnesota (1868) and Nebraska (1871), established coeducational universities. In the Middle States and in the East, the first endeavors to give college education to girls produced separate colleges. Vassar (1865), Smith (1871), Wellesley (1871) and Bryn Mawr (1885) were private schools built for a religious purpose.[30]

This, then, has been and is the development in higher education in America. There exist the private, sectarian schools on the one hand, and the secular, state universities on the other. In their respective fields, both represent a danger to the faith and morals of young Catholic Americans.

---

[30] Thwing, pp. 342-349.

CHAPTER III

General and Special Legislation Concerning the Attendance of Catholics at Non-Catholic Universities and Colleges

Article 1. The Middle Ages to the Council of Trent (1545-1563).

Legislation from the Church to offset the threat of universities and colleges which would serve to endanger or even undermine the faith and morals of Catholic youth had its remote origins in the XV century. In his many condemnations of the Church and its organizations, John Wycliff (1324-1384) included the universities which existed in his time. The Council of Constance (1414-1418) condemned his proposition.[1] The affirmations of John Hus (ca. 1370-1415), who sustained Wycliff, were also condemned by the same Council.[2]

The V General Council of the Lateran (1512-1517) found that the tide of heresy was in the process of quick growth and tried to stem it through legislation for institutions of higher learning. Thus, in its eighth session the Council directed:

> . . . And, since truth does not contradict truth, we declare that every assertion contrary to truth illumined by faith is absolutely false, and to teach otherwise we strictly forbid; and we decree that all who adhere to errors of this kind be avoided and punished as heretics and infidels seeking to de-

[1] Sessio VIII, 4 maii, 1415, n. 29: "Universitates, studia, collegia, graduationes, et magisteria in iisdem sunt vana gentilitate introducta; tantum prosunt Ecclesiae, sicut diabolus."—H. Denzinger-J. Umberg, *Enchiridion Symbolorum Definitionum et Declarationum de Rebus Fidei et Morum* 26 ed., Friburgi Brisgoviae: Herder and Co., 1947), n. 609 (hereafter cited *Enchiridion Symbolorum*).

[2] Sessio XV, 6 iulii, 1415, n. 25—Denzinger, *Enchiridion Symbolorum*, n. 651.

> stroy the Catholic faith. Moreover, we strictly command all professors in universities and other public institutions of learning that when they teach or explain to their students those principles and conclusions in which these false teachers are known to deviate from the truth, namely, the immortality and unity or oneness of the soul, the eternity of the world, etc., they make every effort to offset and refute those false teachings by presenting clearly on those points the truths of the Catholic religion.[3]

Further, no one in holy orders, secular or religious, was to study philosophy and the liberal arts unless, at the same time, he pursued a course of study in theology or canon law. This insistence on the study of theology or canon law was to provide the student with a "means wherewith to cleanse and heal the infected roots of philosophy and poetry." The Council required that its rules be published annually, at the beginning of the school year, by the ordinaries in whose territory the institution was located.[4]

The enactments of the previous Councils had failed to bring about the desired effect. In consequence, when the Council of Trent (1545-1563) was convened it sought to apply a remedy for the great dangers that threatened souls. The bishops clearly set forth their purpose in the second session of the Council.

> . . . Moreover, since it is the chief care, solicitude and intention of this holy council that the darkness of heresies, which for so many years has covered the earth, being dispelled, the light of Catholic truth may, with the aid of Jesus Christ, Who is the true light, shine forth in splendor and purity, and that those things that need reform may be reformed, the council exhorts all Catholics here assembled and who will be here assembled, especially those having a knowledge of the Sacred Scriptures, that by sedulous meditation they ponder diligently within themselves, by what ways and means the

[3] H. Schroeder, *Disciplinary Decrees of the General Councils* (St. Louis: B. Herder and Co., 1937), pp. 487, 488.

[4] *Loc. cit.*

> intention of the council can best be carried out and the desired result obtained; how the thing to be condemned may be condemned more promptly and prudently and those to be approved may be approved, so that throughout the whole world all may with one voice and with the same profession of faith, glorify God and the Father of Our Lord Jesus Christ.[5]

The institutions for higher education were to have an important part in the work of internal reform, and they were to make a contribution to the task of extirpating heresy. The *gymnasia* were to be canonically visited by the local bishops, and with the aid of the local governments they were to institute religious instructions for all students where it had not yet been done. Where religious instruction had been neglected, even though it had already been instituted, it was to be restored. No one was to be admitted to the office of instructor who had not been previously examined by the bishop of the locality as to his life, morals and knowledge.[6] The universities were obliged to teach all matters of Catholic faith in conformity with the canons and decrees of the Council and to pledge themselves by solemn oath each year to carry out the ordinances of the Council.[7]

The course which higher education was to follow was quickly perceived by the local ordinaries. The local councils enacted legislation designed to protect the faithful of all ages against the dangers of heresy and the weakening of morals which threatened those who attended non-Catholic schools and universities. The Council of Augsburg (1548) forbade attendance at such institutions, even though a Catholic should desire to teach rather than study at such schools.[8] The II Council of Cologne (1549) re-

---

[5] H. Schroeder, *Canons and Decrees of the Council of Trent*, p. 13.

[6] Sessio V, *de ref.*, c. 1—Schroeder, p. 25.

[7] Sessio XXV, *de ref.*, c. 2—Schroeder, p. 234.

[8] Cap. 26: "In primis statuimus et ordinamus, ut nullus nostrae Augustensis ditionis aut dioecesis, cujuscumque aetatis, status, ordinis aut gradus fuerit, ad scholas et gymnasia de schismate aut haeresi suspecta, nuperque natis de religione perversis opinionibus contaminata, discendi

quired that all courses in philosophy, law, medicine, theology and Sacred Scriptures be pursued in Catholic schools and universities.[9]

Article 2. The Council of Trent to the III Plenary Council of Baltimore (1884).

The Council of Trent had commanded the bishops and the religious orders to intensify their zeal and interest in higher education, and urged the founding of new Orders which would aid in a great and necessary reform of education on all levels. The leaders of the Reformation had, in the meantime, enlisted the aid of local civil governments in their usurpation of the colleges and universities.[10] From this appeal by the religious leaders of the Reformation was to come the system of education as we know it today in many countries, namely, the state-controlled universities and colleges. Indeed, such was not the idea nor the ideal of the Reformation. Religious education, even though heretical in character, remained part of the prescribed course of study in Germany and in England. Schools were to be institutions still under the control of the particular church of the territory in Germany as dictated by the principle of "Cuius regio eius religio" as set up in the socalled Religious Peace of Augsburg on Sept. 26, 1555. The English civil law required abjurations and oaths from all teachers in support of Anglicanism, and saw to it that both pupils and teachers were examined in their religious beliefs.[11]

---

docendive causa audeat proficisci. Nam qui contra fecerit, is sciat se nobis poenas debitas daturum."—Mansi, XXXII, 1319.

[9] Cap. 2: "Ceterum exacta atque absoluta artium et linguarum cognitio ratioque et reliqua philosophia, physica item et ars medica, jurisprudentia, et theologia seu scriptura sacra, non nisi in probatis academiis, et catholicis universalium studiorum scholis expectentur, doceantur, ac tradantur. . ."—Mansi, XXXII, 1364.

[10] Cf. Luther's letter in Cassidy, *History of Education,* pp. 393, 394.

[11] C. Boffa, *Canonical Provisions for Catholic Schools (Elementary and Intermediate),* The Catholic University of America Canon Law Studies, n. 117 (Washington, D.C.: The Catholic University of America Press, 1939), p. 48 (hereafter cited Boffa).

The acceptance and spread of a philosophy based on naturalism and rationalism, as also the fact that theology lost its primary place in many of the universities in Germany,[12] led eventually to government control and direction. In England the purpose of education had become that of affiliating men with the Anglican Church, for all the courses offered to the student were to prepare him for an apologetic which defended the State-Church. The management of the schools was in the hands of Protestant clergymen, but it was the State which was in charge of education. The Revolution in France, which made the State and Nation supreme in all the political thinking of those in power, and rendered the individual completely subordinate to the aims and ends of the state,[13] was but a final step which prepared the way for the government-controlled university in the early years of the XIX century, in which "academic freedom" had replaced and removed theology and religion.

The early effects of the Reformation had left some universities with only one-quarer of their former enrollment, and had closed many others.[14] The restoration of universities and colleges and their subsequent growth was to take almost a century. The first pieces of legislation were concerned with education on the elementary and intermediate level.[15] For the Catholics of Germany there were Catholic universities at Cologne and Utrecht, and for the English and Irish Catholics a Catholic education could be had in the Catholic universities across the Channel in France and in Belgium, and also in Spain. Tonsured clerics were permitted to attend universities only after their bishops had considered the reasons advanced and had approved the request for permission to

---

[12] Cf. *supra*, pp. 41, 42.

[13] F. De Hovre, *Philosophy and Education* (Tr. by E. Jordan, New York: Benziger Bros. 1931), p. 268.

[14] Paulsen, *German Education*, p. 54; Leach, pt. II, i-v.

[15] S.C. de Prop. Fide, instr. (ad Vic. Ap. Societ. Mission. ad Exteros), a. 1659—*Codicis Iuris Canonici Fontes*, cura Emi Petri Card. Gasparri editi (9 vols., Romae postea Civitate Vaticana: Typis Polyglottis Vaticanis, 1923-1939), n. 4463 (hereafter cites *Fontes*); S. C. S. Off., instr., 29 iul., 1699—*Fontes*, n. 762.

be absent from the diocese.[16] There was no question that the university would be a Catholic university.

The XIX century brought the growing concept of "academic freedom" in higher education into great, practical popularity. Reason had become the acknowledged guide for all university thought and all university practice. "Free scientific research" would make men independent in thought and also give them moral and intellectual freedom.[17] The same century saw the control and direction of education pass into the hands of civil officials in many countries.[18]

The dangers from such a philosophy and such control were most apparent to Pope Pius IX (1846-1878). Accordingly in the early years of his pontificate he began himself, and through the Sacred Congregations, a series of instructions to control the dangers deriving from such a system.

It was during Pius IX's reign that a problem concerning interdenominational schools was presented to the Sacred Congregation for the Propagation of the Faith in 1847. The question was not being presented for the first time, however. In 1841, the Bishops of Ireland had requested norms for a course of action from the Sacred Congregation in the matter of interdenominational schools in Ireland. The Sacred Congregation had answered[19] that it would give no definite judgment, leaving the matter to the conscientious judgment of the bishops. In their deliberations, however, they were to be mindful of certain instructions and recommendations issued by the Sacred Congregation:

(1) All books which were not in accord with the Sacred Scriptures or which were harmful to faith or morals were to be removed. This would not be too difficult, since no existing civil law barred such a request.

---

[16] Innocentius XIII, const. *Apostolic ministerii,* 23 maii, 1723—*Fontes,* n. 280; Benedictus XIII, const. *In supremo,* 23 sept. 1742—*Fontes,* n. 283.

[17] Paulsen, *German Universities,* p. 52.

[18] In Germany in the beginning of the century; in Italy between 1802 and 1811; in France in 1808, and in Austria in 1868. Cf. Boffa, pp. 50, 51.

[19] S.C. de Prop. Fide, litt. (ad Ep. Hiberniae), 16 ian. 1841—*Fontes,* n. 4787.

(2) In schools in which Catholic teachers were students, only Catholics were to teach them religion, history and moral subjects.

(3) In those classes which were common to all students only profane subjects were to be taught with no admixture of truths which were labeled as fundamental to all religions. Sectarian beliefs were to be taught in a place apart from the common classroom, since any other method would be dangerous for Catholic youth.

(4) The bishops and pastors were to exercise vigilance over these schools. This new system of inter-denominational schools was to be carefully discussed in the Provincial Synods, and difficult matters were to be referred to the Holy See.

In 1847, some of the bishops of Ireland had expressed themselves as strongly in favor of the erection of new, Catholic colleges to remove the dangers to the youth of Ireland which came from their attendance at inter-denominational schools. Other bishops thought that the plan was not wise in view of the government controls which would be placed on the new colleges. When the Sacred Congregation for the Propagation of the Faith was given the problem for discussion and solution, it replied[20] that no bishop was to have a part in such a plan, since the dangers to the faith from the government control of such colleges would be multiplied. The sacred Congregation urged that the bishops should, rather, improve and enlarge the Catholic colleges already in existence, and place greater emphasis on the courses in philosophy. Further, the bishops were encouraged to consider plans for the erection of a Catholic university to be modeled after the one at Louvain. The Sacred Congregation assured the bishops that the question was given no final determination by its answer, so that the bishops were free to communicate new evidence and new plans to the Sacred Congregation. When, in 1848, the same question was proposed again,[21] the Sacred Congregation answered that after careful consideration it saw no sufficient reasons for changing its instructions of the previous year, since the dangers to

---

[20] S.C. de Prop. Fide (Hiberniae) 9 oct. 1847—*Fontes,* n. 4820.
[21] S.C. de Prop. Fide (Hiberniae) 11 oct. 1848—*Fontes,* n. 4827.

Catholic youth from colleges under the control of the Anglican government in England still remained. The project which would provide a Catholic university for Ireland was commended by the Sacred Congregation. The completion of such a university should offer an incentive for the zeal of the bishops. Another proposal of the same question to the Sacred Congregation in 1860[22] brought no changes from its former replies.

The pronouncements of Pope Pius IX on the problems facing the Church because of the secular philosophy and method of higher education were clear and frequent. It will serve the reader best, perhaps, to treat the various papal instructions to the bishops of Europe by reason of the nations to which they were addressed rather than in a strictly chronological order. In 1849, Pope Pius IX wrote to the Archbishops and Bishops of Italy[23] to be on their guard so that students in all public and private schools would be educated according to a *ratio studiorum* which was in conformity, in all points, with Catholic doctrine. They were to be taught by teachers who were imbued with real virtue and true religion. They were to be taught to appreciate the necessary safeguards and to recognize and avoid snares and errors, so that they might be true Christians and useful citizens. The bishops were to labor with great firmness of purpose and were to be extremely vigilant in everything that regarded schools and the instruction and education of children and of the youth of both sexes. The enemies of religion and human society labored insidiously and diabolically to pervert the minds and hearts of youth from their earliest years, and their great objective was to withdraw all schools and institutions from the authority of the Church and the vigilance of pastors.

He explained to the Bishops of Sardinia[24] that he deplored the action of the government which excluded the Church by law on October 4, 1848, from any and all authority or control in any schools save seminaries. The bishops were to be without voice in the discipline of universities, in the courses offered for study, in

---

[22] S.C. de Prop. Fide, instr. (ad Archiep. Hiberniae), 7 apr. 1860—*Fontes*, n. 4849.

[23] Pius IX, epist. *Nostis et Nobiscum*, 5 dec. 1849—*Fontes*, n. 508.

[24] Pius IX, allocut. *In consistoriali*, 1 nov. 1850—*Fontes*, n. 509.

the granting of degrees, and in the selection and approval of teachers. They were to be without the right of vigilance in matters of faith or morals. They had excluded all measure of episcopal authority. Many meetings and discussions had proved fruitless, although the Pope had demanded that the civil government was not to enact the prescriptions which were in violation of previous agreements between the Holy See and the government.

The bishops of Sicily were ordered to inspect both public and private schools for youth with great diligence. The Catholic schools were to provide in a way which would ensure that the youth of both sexes were carefully instructed in the fear of God and in His commandments in order to prevent their falling prey to the wiles of the enemies of religion.[25]

In those countries where the Church still maintained some measure of freedom to exercise its proper role in education because of agreements with the civil governments, Pius IX insisted on an exclusively Catholic education for all students. In his allocution to the Hierarchy of Spain[26] there was a definite task assigned to the bishops. The concordat between Spain and the Holy See provided that the studies made in the universities, colleges, seminaries and schools would be in complete accord with Catholic doctrine. The bishops were to be on guard to see to it that a true Christian education was given to youth with no interference from civil authorities. In the public schools the bishops were to be free in the exercise of their pastoral duties.

Frequent synods and councils were urged for Austria by Pius IX to help in the work of neutralizing the dangers from the false teachings in Indifferentism and Rationalism. From their deliberations, the bishops were to provide for the instruction of youth not only in the elements of the faith but also in what amounted to a fuller and more intense religous knowledge. With the help of the faithful, the bishops were to formulate plans for the building of new schools to combat the dangers of perversion and corruption.[27]

In Portugal, where the enemies of the Church were also at

[25] Pius IX, ep. encycl. *Cum nuper,* 20 ian. 1848—*Fontes,* n. 523.

[26] Pius IX, allocut. *Quibus luctuosissimis,* 5 sept. 1851—*Fontes,* n. 512.

[27] Pius IX, ep. encycl. *Singulari quidem,* 17 mart. 1856—*Fontes,* n. 521.

work, the Pope ordered[28] the bishops to be constant in their work of unmasking and pointing out error and condemning evil. In all schools, eternal salvation was to be the *ratio studiorum,* and the bishops were to be sure that all students were carefully instructed in matters of faith and morals.

A new civil regime in the Duchy of Baden in Germany had completed new regulations for all the schools of that territory. As time went on, the rights of the Church to exercise its powers of teaching and of vigilance were in danger of being lost in the neutral schools which were being formed. In a letter to the Archbishop of Freiburg,[29] Pius IX made clear the Church's reasons for the condemnation of such schools. Any *ratio docendi* which was divorced from the Catholic Faith and from the power of the Church could only bring grave harm to students on all levels. Religious education was to be primary in the formation of youth; all other knowledge was but a complement of religious knowledge. The Church had established schools with great care for the precise purpose that the light of faith be not extinguished. In those schools in which the truths revealed by God were denied or were improperly subjected to the examination of human reason, it was inevitable that the proper subjection of natural things to the supernatural order was taken away. In that way men's minds were turned from their eternal end, and their thoughts and actions were confined within the limits of the fleeting, material things of this world. Certainly, in all those places where the plan of education sought to expel the authority of the Church and exposed the faith of students to danger, the Church had but a single course by reason of its divine commission. It could spare neither pains nor sacrifice to provide the necessary Catholic schools and Catholic education, and accordingly it warned all the faithful that in conscience they could not attend the schools opposed to the Catholic Church. The unjust encroachments of the State in usurping the powers of the Church in the matter of education on all levels were numbered by Pius IX among the errors condemned in the *Syllabus* of errors published during his reign.[30]

---

[28] Pius IX, epist., *Quo graviora,* 8 iul. 1862—*Fontes,* n. 535.

[29] Pius IX, epist. *Quum non sine,* 14 iul. 1864—*Fontes,* n. 539.

[30] Denzinger, *Enchiridion Symbolorum,* nn. 1739, 1745.

The absolute condemnations and the simple prohibitions of Pope Pius IX were to bring problems for the bishops in those countries where the education of youth had passed under the control of the State. In 1866 the bishops of Switzerland asked the Sacred Congregation of the Holy Office if it were lawful for parents to permit their children to attend the mixed and neutral schools directed and controlled by the State. The Sacred Congregation held for the principle that, as a general rule, it was unlawful for the parents to do so. In particular cases the ordinary could permit attendance at such schools provided that the bishops, the priests and the parents joined in a concerted effort to remove all the dangers to the faith and morals of the children. Such toleration on the part of the ordinary, the priests and the parents was to be acceptable only after the possibility of sending the children to other areas for a Catholic education had been carefully weighed and considered.[31]

In the next year, the Sacred Congregation for the Propagation of the Faith found it necessary to order the bishops of England to forbid the attendance of Catholics at the universities of Oxford and Cambridge. The teaching of errors and the silence with regard to solid doctrines as also the influence of the other students who in making use of the forces of human respect and ridicule made proximate the occasion for a lapse from faith and morals on the part of Catholic students at both universities. Thus there could be no sufficient reason for the attendance of Catholics in light of the existing conditions, and the bishops were to make the instructions of the Sacred Congregation known through pastoral letters to the clergy and to the people.[32]

The same problem plagued the bishops of some Eastern churches. Thus, in Syria, a notorious apostate had opened a college in Beirut and was trying to make it out to be the national university of Syria. Meanwhile, in a convenient place just outside the city-limits, a college opened by Greek schismatics also sought to give itself the character of a national university. In 1865[33] the Sacred

[31] S.C.S. Off., instr. 21 mart. 1866—*Fontes,* n. 992.

[32] S.C. de Prop. Fide, litt. encycl., 6 aug. 1867—*Fontes,* n. 4868.

[33] S.C. de Prop. Fide, litt. encycl., 20 mart. 1865—*Fontes,* n. 4863.

Congregation ordered the bishops to use all their influence and episcopal authority to prevent the attendance of Catholics, even thought it should require the inflicting of canonical penalties. Further, the bishops were to make haste in the work of erecting Catholic colleges despite the opposition of the schismatics and heretics.

In 1868 the Sacred Congregation warned Oriental bishops about the dangers to Catholic youth from attendance at the schools of schismatics, which had been sanctioned by the civil governments. They were to supervise the selection of books and teachers, and they were to make a careful investigation of governmental policies of direction and control before they accepted any government grants or benefits. These matters were to be investigated and discussed in their provincial councils.[34]

In 1869 the Vicars Apostolic of the East Indies were reminded that Catholics were not to attend schools erected and controlled by the civil government in which the teachers were chosen, books prepared and curricula formed in a way that made no mention of religion or matters of faith. The permission and subsidies granted by the government for the establishment of private schools were to be utilized only when the conditions set by the government were not contrary to faith or morals. Wherever it was possible, the vicars were to erect Catholic schools which would be on an equal plane with the government schools in the matter of instruction and the courses offered.[35]

The mind of the Church was clearly expressed by the end of the reign of Pope Pius IX in 1878. The general principles from which all decisions and instructions of the Holy See would proceed were:

(1) The Church sought and demanded a Catholic education for Catholic students of all ages, even though it should entail sacrifices on the part of the parents.

(2) The Holy See deplored political conditions in any country which permitted the State to exercise the full direction and control of education.

---

[34] S.C. de Prop. Fide, instr., 25 apr. 1868—*Fontes,* n. 4873.

[35] S.C. de Prop. Fide, instr., 8 sept. 1869—*Fontes,* n. 4876.

(3) The attendance of Catholics at schools where the *ratio studiorum* was not in accord with Catholic doctrine was, in general, unlawful.

(4) In those places in which, in the considered judgment of the ordinary, sufficient reasons permitted that the attendance of Catholic students be tolerated in such schools, safeguards were to be provided by the parents and the priests.

(5) The Holy See did and would prohibit the attendance of Catholic students at schools on any level if there were not sufficient reasons and safeguards in view of the dangers to faith and morals to tolerate such attendance.

Pope Leo XIII (1878-1903) with a firm hand and a sure touch placed his finger on the cause of the evils affecting the world at the time of his accession to the papal throne. The last years of Pius IX had been saddened by the persecutions leveled against the Church in many parts of the world. There was disorder in the minds of men, there were abuses in temporal administration, there was private corruption, and there was a false and ruinous Liberalism which proved detrimental to body and soul alike. The cause of the evils of Society in his own time Leo XIII placed in the contempt for the authority of the Church, which had weakened the very foundations of civilization.[36] He pointed out the duties of all bishops in their work for the education of the souls committed to their care. They were to strive that the teachings of the Catholic Faith be implanted early in the souls of the faithful and strike deep root that they might be kept free from the vicious blight of error. All education was to be in complete harmony with the Catholic Faith in its literature and system of teaching, particularly in philosophy, upon which the foundation of the other sciences depends in such great measure.[37]

When the plan for education in Belgium was enacted into law (July, 1880) and when it excluded the authority of the Church in the schools and its right of vigilance, Leo XII complained bitterly[38] that religious education had been barred from the

[36] Leo XIII, ep. encycl., *Inscrutabili,* 21 apr. 1878—*Fontes,* n. 573.

[37] *Loc. cit.*

[38] Leo XIII, allocut. *Summi Pontificatus,* 20 aug. 1880—*Fontes,* n. 581.

curriculum and the system of teaching in all public schools. What was even more dangerous, religious instruction had been exluded from the *normal* schools which provided the teachers for the youth of Belgium.

In England, differences and difficulties between religous superiors and bishops had arisen. For resloving the problems, the Pope insisted that it was the right and the obligation of the bishop, in each diocese, to exercise vigilance over the education of youth, even though some schools in his diocese were under the direction of the religious clergy. Such was to be the rule also for other schools and colleges in which religious had assumed the work of educating youth, unless the particular religious Order enjoyed a privilege of exemption.[39]

The attempt of the civil government in France in 1884 to give to the schools of France a mixed or netural character and curriculum regarding religion and its importance in the courses of study was condemned, and the bishops and the people were counselled to prevent such legislation and to avoid neutral schools.[40]

The condition of education in Hungary had also taken a turn for the worse. The principles of rationalism and naturalism brought great sorrow to the Church as the Parent-Educator. The schools in the country were proceeding along lines which would make them neutral or mixed in character. From education of that kind there could come only a generation of youth absymally ignorant of holy things and without a care for religion. The bishops were to see to it[41] that the parents were warned of the dangers, and that the teachers were carefully chosen. It was also clear that Leo XIII included schools of higher education in his instructions to the bishops concerning their vigilance. Further, they were to move as quickly as possible to the erection of new schools on all levels in which they could see to it that the highest standards were maintained, and in which they could direct and control the curriculum and the manner of teaching.

---

39 Leo XIII, const. *Romanos Pontifices,* 8 maii, 1881—*Fontes* n. 582.

40 Leo XIII, Ep. encycl. *Nobilissima,* 8 febr. 1884—*Fontes,* n. 590.

41 Leo XIII, Ep. encycl. *Quod multum,* 22 aug. 1886—*Fontes,* n. 594.

In 1893[42] he urged the bishops to appoint inspectors who would keep them informed of the conditions in the schools. In their meetings the bishops were to devise ways and means of reducing the dangers that affected the students. In the higher schools, particularly, they were to be vigilant concerning books and teachers, so that they might insist that harmful books and teachers be removed.

In Poland, the plan which would keep the schools supposedly Christian in culture and curriculum while they taught positive error, and encouraged impiety by neglecting to give instruction in the Commandments, was condemned by Leo XIII. He ordered that students were not to attend such schools.[43]

In 1897 Leo XIII repeated to the bishops of Austria, Germany and Switzerland that the chief aim of the Church was to have Catholic schools with competent and approved teachers, with no attendance permitted to non-Catholics. Until that was achieved, the bishops were to present a united front and to speak with one mind of one principle, namely, that religious instruction was not to be just another subject in the curriculum, but that religion was to permeate all education.[44]

In a lengthy Instruction to the Vicars Apostolic of China in 1883, the Sacred Congregatiton for the Propagation of the Faith urged the establishment of schools for the careful training of catechists. The Sacred Congregation desired that colleges should be opened in each of the five vicariates as soon as possible. No infidels or Protestants were to be admitted to these colleges. All desired exceptions to the ruling of the Sacred Congregation were to be reported, along with full particulars, and the Sacred Congregation would give the disposition of each case.[45]

The position of the Church through the centuries is clear. In all

---

42 Leo XIII, Ep. encycl. *Constanti Hungarorum,* 2 sept. 1893—*Fontes,* n. 620.

43 Leo XIII, Ep. encycl. *Caritatis providentiaeque,* 19 mart. 1894—*Fontes,* n. 623.

44 Leo XIII, Ep. encycl. *Militantis Ecclesiae,* 1 aug. 1897—*Fontes,* n. 635.

45 S.C. de Prop. Fide, instr., 18 oct. 1883—*Fontes,* n. 4903.

its answers to questions, in all its condemnations of the violations of the right of the parents to educate their children, in all its defenses of its own rights in the field of education, and in all its exhortations to the faithful the Church points to the dangers from and the constant dissatisfaction with any system of education save the one which provides for a Catholic education for all Catholics.

The reader may be moved, perhaps, to object, at this point, that the Holy See condemned as dangerous the education offered in the schools of Europe and the Far East because the schools were professedly anti-Catholic, and that there need not be the same vigorous claim against the education in most of the universities and colleges in America, since few, if any, American schools are anti-Catholic, but simply neutral in the best American tradition. Even a cursory examination of the sources, however, will show that the American bishops and the Holy See were, from early times, gravely concerned about American higher education as it affected Catholic students.

Bishop Carroll's pastoral letter of 1792 reminded Americans that he "considered the virtuous and Christian instruction of youth as a principal object of pastoral solicitude."[46] The excuse given by many Catholic parents that they could not afford to send their sons to be educated in the Catholic colleges of Belgium and France was met with the opening of Georgetown College in 1791. In the same pastoral letter, Bishop Carroll recommended the college to Catholic parents. After discussing the advantages of a religious education he wrote:

> These being the advantages of a religious education, I was solicitous for the attainment of a blessing so desirable to that precious portion of my flock, the growing generation. A school has been instituted at George-Town, which will continue to be under the superintendence and government of some of my reverend brethren, that is, of men devoted by principle and profession to instruct all, who resort to them, in useful learning, and those of our own religion, in its prin-

[46] P. J. Guilday, *The National Pastorals of the American Hierarchy* (Washington, D.C., 1923), p. 3 (hereafter cited *Pastorals*).

> ciples and duties. I earnestly wish, dear brethren, that as many of you, as are able, would send your sons to this school of letters and virtue. I know and lament, that the expense will be too great for many families, and that their children must be deprived of the immediate benefit of this institution; but indirectly, they will receive it; at least, it may be reasonably expected, that some after being educated at George-Town and having returned into their own neighborhood, will become, in their turn, the instructors of the youths who cannot be sent from home; and, by pursuing the same system of uniting much attention to religion with a solicitude of other improvements, the general result will be a great increase of piety, the necessary consequence of a careful instruction in the principles of faith and Christian morality.[47]

Until this happy announcement by Bishop Carroll, higher education in the English colonies could be obtained only in non-Catholic schools, all of which were denominational but one.[48]

In the year 1829 the Fathers of the I Provincial Council of Baltimore were aware of the danger as the thirty-fourth decree of that Council makes clear:

> We judge it to be absolutely necessary that schools be established in which the young may be taught the principles of faith and morality while they are being instructed in profane matters.[49]

The zeal and devotion which the American bishops brought to their work was not limited to a concern for the erection and multiplication of Catholic institutions of higher learning. They were vigilant also about the textbooks to be used in Catholic colleges.

---

[47] *Ibidem*, p. 4.

[48] Harvard (Puritan), William and Mary and King's College (Anglican), Yale and Dartmouth (Congregational), Princeton (Presbyterian), Brown (Baptist), Rutgers (Dutch Reformed) and Pennsylvania (nondenominational).

[49] *Acta et Decreta Sacrorum Conciliorum, Collectio Lacensis* (7 vols., Friburgi Brisgoviae, (1870-1892), III, 32 (hereafter cited *Coll. Lac.*).

Accordingly in the II Provincial Council of Baltimore (1833) they decreed that the presidents of Georgetown, St. Mary's and Mount St. Mary's should begin the work of preparing suitable textbooks.[50] The Pastoral Letter of 1833 reveals the course of action which was being followed:

> The education of the rising generation is, beloved brethren, a subject of the first importance; and we have accordingly, at all times, used our best efforts to provide, as far as our means would permit, not only ecclesiastical seminaries to insure a succession in our priesthood and its extension; but we have moreover sought to create colleges and schools in which your children, whether male or female, might have the best opportunities of literature and science, united to a strict protection of their morals and the best safeguards of their faith. You are aware that the success and the permanence of such institutions rest almost exclusively with you. It will be our most gratifying duty to see that their superiors and professors are worthy of the high trust reposed in them . . .[51]

A declaration of the dangers to the faith and morals of Catholic students from the Bibles and textbooks in use in non-Catholic colleges, and an exhortation for a truly Catholic higher education were included in the pastoral letter following the IV Provincial Council of Baltimore in 1840:

> Respecting our colleges and schools for males, though much has been effected, yet much remains to be done by their multiplication, and we exhort you for the sake of your children, your country and your religion, to come to our aid for the purpose of making the effort thus to provide for the literary, moral and religious education of one sex as well as of the other. We have exposed to you the danger of their position, we confide in your charity and in your zeal.[52]

---

[50] *Coll. Lac.*, III, 42.

[51] Guilday, *Pastorals*, p. 74.

[52] Guilday, *Pastorals*, p. 135.

The Fathers at the I Plenary Council of Baltimore (1852) saw no lessening of the dangers from a system of education which was not Catholic. The pastoral letter spoke of their great solicitude for the younger members of the flock who were growing up in ignorance of eternal truth and of their religious duties. They put the charge to the parents:

> To avert this evil give your children a Christian education, that is an education based on religious principles, accompanied by religious practices and always subordinate to religious influence. Be not led astray by the false and delusive theories which are so prevalent, and which leave youth without religion, and, consequently, without anything to control the passions, promote the real happiness of the individual, and make society find in the increase of its members, a source of security and prosperity. Listen not to those who would persuade you that religion can be separated from secular instruction. If your children, while they advance in human sciences, are not taught the science of the saints, their minds will be filled with every error, their hearts will be receptacles of every vice and that very learning which they have acquired, in itself so good and so necessary, deprived of all that could shed on it the light of heaven, will be an additional means of destroying the happiness of the child, embittering still more the chalice of parental disappointment, and weakening the foundations of social order. . . . Encourage and support the establishment of Catholic schools; make every sacrifice which may be necessary for this object: spare our hearts the pain of beholding the youth whom, after the example of our Master, we so much love, involved in all the evils of an uncatholic education, evils too multiplied and too obvious to require that we should do more than raise our voices in solemn protest against the system from which they spring. In urging upon you the discharge of this duty, we are acting on the suggestion of the Sovereign Pontiff, who in an encyclical letter, dated 21 November, 1851, calls on all the Bishops of

the Catholic world, to provide for the religious education of youth.[53]

In the II Plenary Council of Baltimore (1866) the bishops recalled and confirmed the practice of inspecting and approving textbooks before they were given to students in schools and colleges.[54]

The III Plenary Council of Baltimore (1884) treated of the Catholic Education of Youth in Title VI of its Decrees.[55] In the introductory part of the Title the Fathers of the Council emphasized the fact that the Church and the world differed in principle on the nature and the end of true education. The spirit of Indifferentism, Naturalism and Materialism had turned men's minds until they were working to take the education of youth from the rightful control of parents and the Church and to surrender it entirely to the State. Others were convinced that the function of education was to impart only secular training, which would give to America a generation of men and women who would hold Christ and his Church in contempt.[56] Therefore, parents were obliged to provide a truly Catholic education for their children in Catholic schools unless, in a particular case, the ordinary should judge that a child could attend a public school. His judgment was to be formed only after a careful consideration of the reason offered and the safeguards to be provided by the parents.[57]

In the higher education of Catholic youth, the Fathers of the Council prayed that God would grant their fondest hope of seeing matters so arranged that Catholic youth could pass from the elementary Catholic schools to the higher Catholic schools in the attainment of their desired goals. Their experience had shown them that the attendance of Catholic youth at non-Catholic colleges too often resulted in a loss of faith and a weakening of morals for these young people.[58] Parents were exhorted to send

---

[53] *Ibidem*, pp. 190, 191.

[54] Decree n. 447—*Coll. Lac.*, III, 519.

[55] *Acta et Decreta Balt. Tertii*, nn. 194-213.

[56] Cf. nn. 194, 195.

[57] Cf. nn. 196, 198.

[58] Utinam jam nunc, quod certo venturum esse speramus, res ita disponi et stabiliri possint, ut juvenes Catholici ex Catholicis scholis elementaribus

their children to the Catholic colleges and academies. In the event that a desired course of study was not offered by the Catholic colleges, and for that reason parents felt constrained to enroll their child in a non-Catholic college, the Council warned the parents of the serious obligation they assumed in making as remote as possible the dangers to the faith and morals of their child.[59]

The Pastoral Letter of 1884 recalled that some of the American bishops had participated in the Council of the Vatican (1869). After outlining the work of that Council, the letter in clear, unmistakable terms defined the dangers from the secular education given in non-Catholic colleges at the end of the XIX century in America.

> We have no reason to fear that you, beloved brethren, are likely to be carried away by these or other false doctrines condemned by the Vatican Council, such as materialism or the denial of God's power to create, to reveal to mankind His hidden truths, to display by miracles His almighty power in this world which is the work of His hands. But neither can we close our eyes to the fact that teachers of skepticism and irreligion are at work in our country. They have crept into the leading educational institutions of our non-Catholic fellow-citizens, they have (though rarely) made their appearance in the public press and even in the pulpit. Could we rely fully on the innate good sense of the American people

---

in Catholicas scholas superiores intrare et per eas ad metam desideriorum suorum accurrere possint. Nimis frequenter enim accidit, ut ii qui pueri pii ac puri e sinu familiae Christianae et de sub tecto scholae Catholicae in collegia acatholica transeunt, scientia quidem inflati, caritate vero, i.e, fide modibusque Christianis privati revetantur. —N. 208.

59 . . . parentes in Domino hortamur, ut adolescentes suos, quibus, scholis parochialibus absolutis, superiorem educationem procurare velint, in Catholicas scholas superiores jam nunc existentes mittant. Si vero scholae Catholicae filiis suis pro speciali quem sequuntur studiorum cursu desint eosque ob hanc causam in scholas acatholicas mittere cogantur, enixe eos monemus, ut fidei morumque pericula a filiis suis quam longissime removeant, verbi Domini semper memores: "Quid prodest homini, si mundum universum lucretur, animae vero suae detrimentum patiatur." (Matth., XVI, 26).—N. 210.

> and on that habitual reverence for God and religion which has so far been their just pride and glory, there might seem comparatively little danger of the general diffusion of those wild theories which reject or ignore Revelation, undermine morality, and end not infrequently by banishing God from His own creation. But when we take into account the daily signs of growing unbelief, and see how its heralds not only seek to mould the youthful mind in our colleges and seats of learning, but are also actively working amongst the masses, we cannot but shudder at the dangers that threaten us in the future.[60]

The answer for the problem was the same in America as in any other country. Catholic schools were to be multiplied and perfected. The multiplication was to continue until every Catholic child in America had within its reach the acquisition of a Catholic education. The perfection of Catholic schools was to proceed until they were in no way inferior to any other schools in educational excellence.[61]

A few years after the close of the II Plenary Council of Baltimore, Pope Leo XIII outlined the chief duties of Christians as citizens. He reminded all the faithful that in the administration of Christian affairs, the summit of pontifical power is vested in the Roman Pontiff. Immediately under him are the Bishops. Each bishop is a *master-worker,* since each one of them administers a particular church in the *Spiritual Edifice,* and each had members of the clergy to share his duties and carry out his decisions. This is the unchangeable constitution of the Church, and every one must regulate his conduct in accordance with that constitution. Then follows an exhortation to the heads of families to govern their households according to these precepts and to be solicitous always for the right training of their children. Their right to train their children brings with it the obligation of shaping and directing the education of their children to the end for which God has given them the privilege of transmitting the gift of life. First and fore-

---

[60] Guilday, *Pastorals,* p. 230.

[61] *Ibidem,* pp. 246, 247.

most it is incumbent upon parents that they keep their children away from schools where there is the risk of their drinking in the poison of impiety. *Where the right education of youth is concerned, no amount of trouble or labor can be undertaken, how great soever, but that even greater still may not be called for.*[62]

In a letter to the Bishops of the Province of New York in 1892, Pope Leo XIII expressed the hope that the civil authorities would recognize that the bishops felt it their duty to turn Catholic children away from the schools in which they would receive no religious instruction and in which their morality would be endangered. He urged them to comprehend the necessity of enacting laws which would give assurance to Catholics, who carry their shares of the expense of public instruction, that they would be given an education compatible with their religion. He expressed his confidence in the equity of Americans, and declared his hope that in the United States the Catholic parents would not be obliged to support colleges and schools of which they could not avail themselves for the education of their children.[63]

There were dangers to Catholic faith and morals in American non-Catholic higher education from colonial days to the end of the XIX century. They were recognized and pointed out as real and frightening by the Holy See and by the bishops of the Church in America. Parents and bishops could tolerate the attendance of Catholics at such universities and colleges only if there was a sufficient reason. The sufficient reason was limited by the III Plenary Council of Baltimore to one, namely, the lack of a certain course of study in the Catholic colleges. Coupled with the sufficient reason was the obligation of the parents to provide safeguards against the dangers to the faith and to the morals of such students.

---

[62] Leo XIII, Litt. encycl. *Sapientiae christianae,* 10 ian. 1890—*Fontes,* n. 605.

[63] Leo XIII, ep. *Quae coniunctim,* 23 maii, 1892—*Fontes,* n. 614.

PART II

CANONICAL COMMENTARY

CHAPTER IV

The Present Prohibition.

The present legislation in canon 1374 crystallizes the position held by the Church through the centuries. The great desire of the Church in the important matter of education is expressed in the motto which Pope Pius XI included in his encyclical letter, *Divini illius Magistri*: "Catholic education in Catholic schools for all the Catholic youth."[1] The original and solitary efforts of the Church in the establishment and sanction of organizations and institutions for the higher education of youth were pointed toward the achievement of that end. The subsequent struggles on the part of the popes, the bishops, and also the people against the encroachments of heretics and civil governments sought the same goal. This goal has not been realized in the present, so that the continued existence of dangers from any other system of education for Catholic youth—a fact so clear to the Church in light of the natural law—must even more intensely be clarified for the faithful. Hence there is enacted the present legislation:

> "Pueri Catholici scholas acatholicas, neutras, mixtas, quae nempe etiam acatholicis patent, ne frequentent."[2]

Article 1. The Term *Pueri* and Its Meaning in the Field of Higher Education.

It seems best to the writer that the meaning of *pueri* be treated first because of the disagreement among canonists concerning the extension of the word in the field of higher education.[3] It is a prin-

[1] *AAS,* XXII (1930), 78.

[2] Can. 1374.

[3] Cf. e.g., De Meester, *Iuris Canonici et Iuris Canonico-Civilis Compendium* (3 vols. in 4, Brugis, Desclée, 1921-1928), III (1928), pars I, 231; Mörsdorf,, *Die Rechtssprache des Codex Iuris Canonici* (Paderborn,

ciple of law that a doubtful law does not bind, and this principle is applied in the Code by the supreme legislator.[4] If, then, to extend and to apply the first provision of canon 1374 to Catholic students who desire to attend non-Catholic universities and colleges gives rise to a doubt of law (*dubium iuris*), the prohibition of canon 1374 may not be applied to such students.

It is the opinion of the writer, however, that when such a disagreement among authors occurs the premature application of canon 15 is the first and, in some cases, the only remedy proposed as a scientific solution for the matter in question. Now, it must be remembered that doubt or uncertainty about an existing law is harmful to society and to its members. It is to be expected, then, that legislators and canonists will recognize every instance of this and that they will try, when framing the law, to prevent the incorporation of words and expressions which will create doubts, or seek, when doubts have already arisen, to provide means for their removal. For this purpose it is required that the law evince clear texts only, for these texts state the law through the use of words and propositions. Because of human weakness and erroneous explanations such clarity is not always achieved, so that those who are in need of the clarity remain in their need.

In the Code the legislator has made provision in order that a doubt of law might not arise from any ambiguity or obscurity resulting from his choice of words in the texts which state the law. He has furnished some general norms, so that there might be certitude concerning the given law, even though the text should contain some ambiguous or obscure words. The norms are stated

---

Fried. Schöningh, 1937), p. 116, note 117, and Regatillo, *Institutiones Iuris Canonici* (2 vols., Santander: Sal Terrae, 1942), II, n. 226, all of whom favor the extension of the term, but cf., e.g., Blat, *Commentarium Textus Codicis Iuris Canonici* (5 vols. in 6, Romae, Collegio Angelico, 1919-1927), III, pars. IV, n. 257; Wernz-Vidal, *Ius Canonicum ad Codicis Norman Exactum* (7 toms. in 8 vols., Tom. IV, Vol. II, Romae, Apud Aedes Universitatis Gregorianae, 1935), IV, n. 674 (hereafter cited *Ius Canonicum*), and Bouscaren-Ellis, *Canon Law, A Text and Commenary* (2. ed. Milwaukee, Bruce & Co., 1951), p. 698, who are opposed to such an interpretation.

[4] Can. 15.

in canons 19, 23, 6, n. 4 and 15. These norms are to be used in such cases wherein a doubt of law remains even after the other means provided in the Code by the legislator have been used, namely, the norms as stated in canons 17, 18, and 22. There is an order, then, in the application of the general norms of the Code. Thus, canon 6, n. 4, is not to be invoked unless the previous application of canons 19 and 22 is not *ad rem* or, unless, upon their application, these canons do not provide certitude about the law in question. Then, before canon 15 becomes applicable, it must be clear that canon 6, n. 4, leaves the interpreter of the law without certitude. Canon 15, then, is the final remedy for dispelling a doubt and gaining a certified understanding of an existing law.

In the light of these considerations, the words, *leges in dubio iuris non urgent,* as stated in canon 15, are the expression of the legislator seeking to certify effectively the meaning of the law when a doubt of law actually exists. That a doubt of law does exist, however, can be concluded only after the means provided in canons 17, 18 and 22 have brought no certainty, and when the subsequent application of the norms stated in canons 19, 23, and 6, n. 4, has likewise failed to clarify the meaning of the law.[5]

The doubt of law, then, must be a positive doubt and an objective doubt before an acceptable, juridic application of canon 15 to a given law becomes permissible. The doubt will be positive when motives for doubting are present. Thus, it implies fairly equal reasons for affirming and for denying assent to either proposition or, as St. Thomas remarked: "There is an apparent equality of motives moving the mind to either consideration."[6]

Doubt is objective when there is something really present in the law to correspond to the doubt existing in the mind. It is subjective when it exists in the mind alone, without a correspond-

[5] Bender, "Dubium Iuris in Canone 15," *Ephemerides Iuris Canonici* (Romae, 1945—), XI, (1955), 9, 10.

[6] S. Thomas Aquinas, *Quaestiones Disputatae,* I, *De Veritate* (cura et studio P. Fr. Raymundi Spiazzi, O.P., 8. ed. revisa, Taurini-Romae: Marietti, 1949), q. 14, a.l. "Quandoque (intellectus) non inclinatur magis ad unum quam ad aliud . . . propter apparentem aequalitatem eorum quae movent ad utramque partem."

ing basis in reality or in the nature of things. The doubt will be objective when the positive motives which are proposed are such that they are based on reality. Objective doubt has its cause in an objective thing or in the law itself as stated in the Code. For this reason, the doubt is present independently of canonists and jurists. The law will be said to be doubtful if it is such that of and by itself (*ex se*) it causes doubt, or under its present circumstances give rise to doubt and uncertitude about a right or an obligation which it states or establishes, namely, for persons who study it attentively, see and know its implication, and thereupon try to interpret it.[7]

There is no question that canon 1374 in its first provision is a prohibitory law. The question of doubt, then, must revolve about the extension of that positive prohibitory law to students who seek to further their education in universities and colleges. Only after a proper use of the means of interpretation provided in the Code by the legislator, can one conclude with certainty that a doubt of law exists. This conclusion one can reach only when with reason one can show that the meaning of the law, which employs the word *pueri* in various senses, as extending also to those who are eligible for admission to universities and colleges remains in positive, objective doubt. In the supposition that a canonist entertains such a doubt, the Code insists that he follow the procedure outlined in the canons treating of the interpretation of law.

The presence of an authentic interpretation by the Pontifical Commission for the Authentic Interpretation of the Code[8] would provide the certitude which would remove all doubt. But, no such interpretation has come. Canon 17, therefore, cannot be invoked for the solution which must be sought if there be a positive, objective doubt with regard to the extension or the comprehension of the term *pueri.*

---

[7] Bender, *ibid.*, p. 11.

[8] Pope Benedict XV gave the public power of authoritative interpretation of the canons of the Code exclusively to this special committee, which he established himself in the *Motu Proprio, Cum iuris canonici,* 15 sept. 1917.—*AAS*, IX (1917), 483, 484.

Before a private interpreter of the law proceeds to the application of canon 18 in determining the meaning of what he considers to be a doubtful law, he realizes that he is leaving the field of public and authentic interpretation in the strict sense. He still has at his service, however, the authoritative Instructions which the Holy See may have issued. Upon the appearance of the present Code, decrees general in character were not to be enacted and hence, unless it was otherwise indicated, there was not to be new legislation, nor were the issued directives to be the equivalent of formal, strict, authentic interpretations of the law.[9] The Directives and Instructions of the Sacred Congregations were, nevertheless, to be authoritative "complements to the canons" in the form of administrative regulations and explanations which would determine the practice which the Holy See desired to be followed in order that the prescriptions of the canons might be duly understood and observed.[10]

The first norm of canon 18 requires that the proper, technical, juridical meaning of *pueri* be sought out and explained in the light of the text and context of canon 1374. Once it is found how elsewhere this word has been defined, it must be presumed that the word *pueri* will have the same juridical meaning in canon 1374, unless that meaning is excluded by the text and context of canon 1374. The juridic determination of the extension of the term *pueri* is indeed to be found in canon 88, § 3, but, since the term is limited in that canon to children who have not yet reached the age of reason, it provides no help in the matter at hand. The meaning of the term may, however, also be determined from the usual, natural meaning of the word as it has come down through the centuries, and particularly from the usual meaning of the term at the time when the present law was promulgated. The historical

---

9 *Ibidem*, p. 483.

10 Sacrae Romanae Congregationes *nova Decreta Generalia* iam nunc ne ferant, nisi qua gravis Ecclesiae universae necessitas aliud suadeat. Ordinarium igitur earum munus in hoc genere erit tum curare ut Codicis praescripta religiose serventur, tum *Instructiones*, si res ferant, edere, quae iisdem Codicis praeceptis maiorem et lucem afferant et efficientiam pariant.—*Ibidem*, p. 483.

material of the discussions prior to the promulgation of the Code are not available to the writer. It is not, however, impossible for that reason to determine the meaning that was attached to the word *pueri* by the Legislator when he enacted the law.

In Roman times, the Latin term *puer* had no fixed meaning in the writings of the classical authors. Thus, Plautus (d. circa 186 B.C.) used *puer* in speaking of young males even though they had passed their seventeenth year.[11] Cicero (106-43 B.C.) used the term of young men in their eighteenth or nineteenth year.[12] In the time of Ovid (43-17 B.C.) *puer* was used of young men who were not yet married.[13]

In Roman Law, the term *puer* was not a technical term and it did not indicate a specific age.[14] In the matter of designating the legal status of people by reason of difference in age, the Church usually followed the Roman Law. Thus, to the age of *seven* a person was *infans;* to the age of *fourteen, impubes;* to the age of *twenty-five, minor; after* the age of *twenty-five, major.*[15] A solution to a problem of penal law, as given by Pope Gregory IX (1227-1241)[16] after a case had been appealed to him by the Abbot of St. Remy, serves to throw some light on the nature of the term *pueri.* Since the boy (*puer*) was only 10 years of age, the Pope decided that the Abbot's demand for a monetary settlement from the father of the boy did not have to be met. Hostiensis (d. 1271), in his commentary on the passage, noted that Gregory IX made a distinction in penal matters between boys who were below the age of fourteen and those (*pueri*) who had already passed that age.[17] Reiffenstuel (1642-1703), in treating of the same ruling, included under the term *pueri* as many as four classes of youth.[18]

---

[11] *Truculentus,* 2, 5, 1.

[12] *Ad Familiares,* 2, 12.

[13] *Fasti,* 4, 226.

[14] Cf. Berger, *Encyclopedic Dictionary of Roman Law* (The American Philosophical Society, Philadelphia, 1953), p. 661.

[15] Wernz, *Ius Decretalium,* VI (1913), n. 20.

[16] C. 2, X, *de delictis puerorum,* V, 23.

[17] Cardinalis Hostiensis (Henricus de Segusia), *In Quinque Decretalium Commentaria* (5 vols. in 4, Venetiis, 1570), V, fol. 64, sub 4.

[18] Infantes: Pueri infantiae proximi; Pueri pubertati proximi; Pueri

The V General Council of the Lateran (1512-1517), which, in its disciplinary decrees, insisted on the reform of formal education on all levels, referred to students in several ways. They were called *auditores, pueri* and *adolescentes.*[19] The Council of Augsburg (1548), when speaking of the Decrees of the V General Council of the Lateran which had ordered the erection of schools, used the term *iuventus* when it spoke of the needs of the student.[20] In its instructions to the Vicars Apostolic laboring in the mission territories, the Sacred Congregation for the Propagation of the Faith used a general terminology to designate all those who were at an age which required that they be educated in schools, i.e., *"iuventutem illarum regionum."*[21] The use of a general, rather than of a specific, fixed term was in the answer of the same Sacred Congregation to a question from the missionaries in China in 1838, namely, *adolescentes.*[22] In a letter sent to the Bishops of Ireland in 1841, the use of various words in reference to an identical group of students is evident. When the Sacred Congregation for the Propagation of the Faith made mention of the plans of the civil government to institute inter-denominational schools in Ireland, it referred to these plans with the phrase *"erudiendae iuventutis systemate,"* and, in its warnings against mixed classes, it declared *"Ita enim cum pueris agere periculosum valde videtur."*[23] When matters concerning Catholics of the Oriental Rites were still in the competence of the Sacred Congregation for the Propagation of the Faith, the Oriental bishops were urged to use all

---

Minores.—*Ius Ecclesiasticum Universum* (7 vols., ed. by V. Pelletier, Parisiis, 1864-1870), Lib. I, tit. XXIII, nn. 1, 2, 3, 5.

[19] *Sessio VIII*—Mansi, XXXII, 842; *Sessio IX*—Mansi, XXXII, 881.

[20] Mansi—XXXII, 1319.

[21] S.C. de Prop. Fide, instr. (ad Vic. Ap. Societ. Mission. ad Exteros), a. 1659: "Scholas ubique summa cura et diligentia erigite, et iuventutem illarum regionum gratis docete . . . et conemini quoque ut nullus catholicus tradat filios infidelibus erudiendos, sed vobis vestrisque."—*Fontes,* n. 4463

[22] S.C. de Prop. Fide (C.P. pro Sin.), 19 iul. 1838: "Omnino prohibeantur Christiani adolescentes paganorum scholas frequentare, attento periculo perversionis et idolatriae."—*Fontes,* n. 4473.

[23] S.C. de Prop. Fide, litt. (ad Ep. Hiberniae), 16 ian. 1841—*Fontes,* n. 4787.

their influence to keep the Catholic youth, *"buon numero giovani cattolici di rito orientale,"* from enrolling in and attending certain universities and colleges.[24] The Sacred Congregation of the Holy Office, in treating the problem created for the Catholic Bishops of Switzerland by the mixed schools in their dioceses, spokes of mixed classes for students as a *"contagio, quorum corrupti mores, indita ex sectario dogmate indocilitas. quaeque pueriles animas vehentissime movet, in catholicam fidem atque Ecclesiae praecepta mordax dicacitas, si quid incorruptum, aut firmum in ipsis manserit, labefactent ac perdant necesse est."* In the same Instruction the influence of the teachers in such schools was characterized as an *"auctoritas quippe praeceptorum quae maxime in adolescentium animis valet* . . .[25] When the Sacred Congregation for the Propagation of the Faith declared, in 1867, that the conditions prevalent in the universities at Oxford and Cambridge made the attendance of Catholics at those universities all but indefensible, the Sacred Congregation referred to the young men as *"catholica iuventus"*, and indicated that they would face dangers to their faith and morals from the *"levitas ingenii atque instabilitas adolescentium."*[26] The same Sacred Congregation issued an Instruction to the Vicars Apostolic of the five ecclesiastical regions in China after examining the decrees of their synods. In those parts of the lengthy Instruction that dealt with the education of Catholic youth on all levels, the Sacred Congregation employed the terms *pueri, soboles fidelium, adolescentes, alumni* and *puellae* when it made reference to students.[27] In 1884, the dangers to Catholics from the Masonic influence were pointed out by Pope Leo XIII in his Encyclical *Humanum genus.* [28] The Sacred Congregation of the Holy Office was commissioned by the Pope to spell out in detail the areas of influence and the means to be em-

[24] S.C. de Prop. Fide, litt. (ad Ep. Orient.), 20 mart. 1865—*Fontes,* n. 4863.

[25] S.C.S. Off., instr. 21 mart. 1866—*Fontes,* n. 992.

[26] S.C. de Prop. Fide, litt. encycl. (ad Ep. Angliae), 6 aug. 1867—*Fontes,* n. 4868.

[27] S.C. de Prop. Fide, instr. (ad Vic. Ap. Sin.), 18 oct. 1883—*Fontes,* n. 4903.

[28] 20 apr. 1884—*Fontes,* n. 591.

ployed in the efforts to be made toward the eradication of the evil. In the field of education, all students were embraced in the Sacred Congregation's Instruction to the bishops in the following provisions: *Atque ad inventutem quod attinet . . . ut a teneris annis . . .in scholis ad christianam fidem christianosque mores accurate informentur . . .*[29] The III Plenary Council of Baltimore (1884) used the term *pueri* when speaking of college students.[30] In 1900, the Bishop of Jassy in Roumania wrote to the Sacred Congregation of the Holy Office for a solution to his difficulty occasioned by the circumstances in his diocese. Many non-Catholics sought admission to the Catholic grade-schools and the Catholic high-schools and colleges, and he was concerned about the policy which he should follow. The Sacred Congregation's Instruction referred to the students as *alumni* and *adolescentes.*[31] Pope St. Pius X, in his Encyclical on Catechettical Instruction, spoke of Catholic youth in general terms: *"Tridentina Synodus . . . addit namque teneri parochos . . . per se vel per alios in fidei veritatibus erudire pueros . . ."* For the catechist, no matter what might be his native talents, the rule was: . . . *"numquam se de christiana doctrina ad pueros vel ad populum cum animi fructum esse dicturum, nisi multa commentatione paratum atque expeditum."*[32]

The usual meaning of *pueri* in the documents outlined above was a general rather than a restricted or particular one; it was not limited to any certain age group or to a certain level of the school population. The end and the circumstances of the law, as also the mind of the legislator, are now further indicated in the Code by the fact that under the single title, *De Scholis,* all levels of education are discussed and provided for. The danger of a for-

---

29 S.C.S. Off., instr., 10 maii, 1884—*Fontes,* n. 1085.

30 Nimis frequenter enim accidit, ut ii qui pueri pii ac puri e sinu familiae Christianae et de sub tecto scholae Catholicae in collegia acatholica transeunt . . . *Acta et Decreta,* n. 208.

Pro rerum nostrarum adiunctis et civilis societatis in his regionibus permistione saepe contingit, ut parentes acatholici pueros et puellas suas nostris scholis superioribus committant . . . *Acta et Decreta,* n. 213.

31 S.C.S. Off., instr. (ad Ep. Iassien.), 22 aug. 1900—*Fontes,* n. 1245.

32 S. Pius X, Litt. encycl., *Acerbo nimis,* 15 apr. 1905, n. 11; n. 18—*Fontes,* n. 666.

mal education which is not a Catholic education in a Catholic school is prohibited in only one place, namely, in the enacted provision of canon 1374. To maintain that the legislator does not intend to embrace all Catholic youth in his prohibition is to hold that he makes no provisions for those who have passed through the grades of the elementary schools. The general meaning of *pueri catholici,* as drawn from the documents of the pre-Code law, makes it possible for the legislator to give expression to the end for which he enacted his prohibition in canon 1374. His primary intention in the matter of Catholics attending non-Catholic, neutral, or mixed schools is a prohibition which embraces all those who have not yet completed their formal education.[33]

The final argument for the acceptance of *pueri catholici* as a general expression proceeding from the mind of the legislator is drawn from canon 6, n. 4.[34] From this norm of interpretation established in the Code by the legislator, it is manifest that the new codification of Canon Law did not bring about a complete renovation such as some had perhaps expected. Rather, the Code presupposes the continuity and the progressive development of Canon Law over the years, and only in rare instances does it work a complete change. A partial reflection of the law in force at the time of the promulgation of the Code is contained in the annotations or footnotes of the canons. The notation of the sources in the footnotes is not authentic, nor is it exclusive. The sources in the citations, however, are most servicable to the interpreter of the law in the Code as another form of disclosing the legislator's mind. They are a means of knowing the content of the earlier law. From among the many sources in the footnote to canon 1374, three of the sources contained in the *Collectanea Sacrae Congregations de Propaganda Fide*[35] clearly show that university and

[33] Cf. Vermeersch, "Quinam sunt pueri de quibus in can. 1373, § 1, et 1374?" *Periodica de Re Canonica et Morali,* Brugis (1905—); ab anno 1927; *Periodica de Re Canonica, Morali, Liturgica,* Brugis (1927-1936) et Romae (1937—), XVII (1928), 145*—148* (hereafter cited *Periodica*).

[34] In dubio num aliquid canonum praescriptum cum veteri iure discrepet, a veteri iure non est recedendum.

[35] 2 vols., Vol. I, ann. 1622-1866, nn. 1-1299; Vol. II, ann. 1867-1906,

college students were included among the ones embraced in the prohibition of the canon in the Code.[36] It is true that the old legislation of itself has no juridical value today. It is however, a subsidiary source of the new law when the Code has embodied it in the canons, giving the pre-Code law legal value as an interpreter of the Code law itself.[37]

Thus, for those who would hold that the prohibitory part of canon 1374 must be considered as providing the interpreter of the law with a positive doubt as to the inclusion of students on the university and college level, the prescription of canon 6, n. 4 must be invoked. In the supposition that such a doubt does exist, the Code gives a definite rule. It establishes a presumption in favor of the earlier law. It is not a rejuvenation of that law in this instance, but rather a return to a more seasoned interpretation, or an appeal to an interpretation which is certain. The presumption stated in the law is that the Code has materially retained the earlier law in its prescriptions, so that accordingly any change from the earlier law must be proved. In the light of this presumption, then, even though a positive doubt were established concerning the meaning of *pueri catholici,* so that neither side had moral certitude for its contention because of the presence of equal motives for affirming or denying that the term includes university and college students, the interpreter is not free to depart from the meaning of the term as it was employed in the earlier law.[38]

For the writer, the evidence afforded by the pre-Code documents and writers establishes that in the Latin the term *pueri* was indefinite and generic in its meaning. When used in reference to students, it embraced students on all levels of education. It had

---

nn. 1300-2317, Romae, Typographia Polyglotta S. C. de Propaganda Fide, 1907 (hereafter cited *Collectanea*).

[36] Nn. 1271; 1312; 1329.

[37] Neuberger, *Canon 6 or the Relation of the Codex Iuris Canonici to Preceding Legislation,* The Catholic University of America Canon Law Studies, n. 44 (Washington, D.C., The Catholic University of America, 1927), p. 71.

[38] Van Hove, *Commentarium Lovaniense in Codicem Iuris Canonici* (1 vol. in 5 tomes, Tom. II [*De Legibus Ecclesiasticis*], Mechliniae, H. Dessain, 1930), n. 59.

no fixed, restricted meaning. With the generic meaning it had in the earlier law the term was incorporated in the Code of Canon Law in the one place in which the legislator enacted a prohibition against the attendance of Catholic youth at any school save a Catholic one. In so doing, the legislator did not give rise to any certain, substantial contrariety to the earlier law, nor did he provide the material from which a positive, objective doubt might be raised against the prescriptions of the former legislation. In the work of codification, the codifiers had for their purpose a succinct systematization of the law. It was necessary, therefore, to put aside the narrative and lengthy dispositive expressions found in the former discipline. In some cases, certainly, a reconstruction of this sort provided for a difference in terminology. This is not true, however, with reference to the prohibition enacted in canon 1374. The law and the expression of it was clear. Among the several, general terms in use, the codifiers chose *pueri,* and the legislator made it his own. In so doing, he stated the prohibition and made it applicable to all Catholic youth who are yet in the process of acquiring a formal education, i.e., to all those who are to be instructed in elementary schools, high-schools, colleges and universities.[39]

Article 2. The Meaning of Non-Catholic Universities and Colleges (*Acatholica, Neutra, Mixta*).

The legislator proceeds from the fundamental principle that the necessary religious instruction of Catholic youth, which must permeate the entire period of their formal education, cannot be had in any school but a truly Catholic one. For this reason he must and he does prohibit the attendance of Catholic youth at any non-Catholic school. In the light of the experience of his predecessors with the growth of Naturalism, Indifferentism and Secularism in the educational policies of the many civil governments which had

[39]Meyer, *Institutions Iuruis Naturalis* (2 vols., Friburgi Brisgoviae, 1900) II, 732; Mörsdorf, *Die Rechtssprache des Codex Iuris Canonici,* p. 116; Guay, "Fréquentation des Ecoles Non-Catholiques," *Revue de l'Université d'Ottawa,* VII (1937), 33*-48*.

usurped the rights of parents and the rights of the Church, and in keeping with their frequent condemnations of the schools evolved from such a system, the legislator makes specific determination of the schools embraced in his prohibition. He exhausts the possibilities and the ramifications of any system of education which is not the Catholic one. He classifies all the schools prohibited for Catholic youth under three general headings. The basis for his division is the manner in which the necessity of instruction in our holy religion is received by the school authorities and imparted to their students. The first division is an obvious one. There are schools which are opposed to the Catholic religion, so that their religious instruction is anti-Catholic in character, or there may be schools which are non-Catholic in that they give to their students a course of instruction in a heretical, schismatic or pagan religion. These schools are embraced in the legislator's designation of *scholas acatholicas*.[40]

The Protestant Reformation provided the occasion for the growth of the second type of school which falls under the prohibition of canon 1374. As traced in a previous chapter of this work,[41] the virtual surrender of the task of providing education by the leaders of the Reformation to the civil authorities paved the way for a system of education which would be divorced from the initiative and the control of the parents and the Church, and which would turn its energies and efforts to producing citizens for the State only. Such a system would keep itself aloof from and unhampered by the religious differences of ecclesiastics and divines. It would, in short, remain neutral in the matter of formal religious instruction of any kind. In the colleges and universities which have espoused this form of neutrality, there is no attempt to impart any religious instruction. These schools pursue a course contrary to the fundamental principles of education. "They cannot long remain neutral, since as a matter of fact they soon become irreligious."[42] The students at such schools are not given neutral

---

[40] Wernz-Vidal, *Ius Canonicum*, IV, n. 675.

[41] Ch. III, Art. 2.

[42] Pius XI, Litt. encycl. *Divini illius Magistri*, 31 dec. 1929—*AAS*, XXII (1930), 76.

textbooks. They are not taught neutral or indifferent sciences or courses by neutral teachers. In the event that, for the present, such schools, neutral in the matter of courses and teachers, actually do exist in given places, they succeed only in removing religion from the lives of their students while promoting error and a spirit hostile to religion. These are the prohibited *scholae neutrae* of canon 1374.[43]

The final possibility—that of schools of a mixed character—is realized in those colleges and universities which admit students of any religious denomination or of no religious denomination, and in which formal religious instruction is given in some degree or other to the students of the different religious persuasions. The religious instruction, as part of the curriculum, may assume different characteristics and methods in the different institutions. Thus, in one, the tenets of the many beliefs represented in the student-body may be taught to many, separate groups. In another, the principles and beliefs labeled as common to all religions may be taught to all the students in the same manner, and by the same lecturer, perhaps.[44] These are the *scholae mixtae* mentioned in canon 1374.

It should be noted here that a Catholic college or university which permits non-Catholics to become part of its student-body is not to be considered as a prohibited school.[45] Nor does the canon intend to include those institutes, improperly called schools, which have as their sole purpose the giving of instruction which will enable those in attendance to acquire a particular skill. They make no attempt to educate in the formal sense. Such institutes

---

[43] Coronata, *Institutiones Iuris Canonici* (5 vols., Vol. II, 4. ed. Taurini, Marietti, 1951), II, n. 947 (hereafter cited *Institutiones*).

[44] The mind of the Church on "co-educational" colleges and universities which admit and train young men and women on a plane of absolute equality, with no allowances or considerations for their natural differences and temperaments, is clear. There is no canon in the Code which treats specifically of the question, but the position of the Church is that they are dangerous and harmful to Christian education. Cf. Pius XI's encyclical *Divini illius Magistri*—*AAS*, XXII (1930), 72.

[45] Vermeersch-Creusen, *Epitome Iuris Canonici* (3 vols., Vol. II, 7. ed., Mechliniae-Romae, H. Dessain, 1954), II, n. 711 (hereafter cited *Epitome*).

would be, for example, schools for the training of typists, of auto mechanics, or of television repair experts. All confusion between such institutes and the so-called Technical Colleges and Universities which do offer a full course of formal studies to complement the instruction given in particular technical skills must be avoided. These latter are colleges and universities in the sense of institutions offering a formal education to their students, and hence they may well fall into one of the prohibited classes of schools outlined above.

The dangers to the faith and morals of Catholic youth in such colleges and universities have been enumerated and explained by the Holy See as coming from the teachers,[46] from the curriculum[47] and from the association and daily companionship with students who are not Catholics.[48]

The prohibition of canon 1374 extends, then, to any college and university which, being non-Catholic in view of its character as a *schola acatholica, neutra* or *mixta,* cannot fulfill the requirements of the Church as expressed by Pope Pius XI:

> The proper and immediate end of Christian education is to cooperate with divine grace in forming the true and perfect Christian, that is, to form Christ Himself in those regenerated by baptism, according to the emphatic expression of the Apostle: "My little children, of whom I am in labor again, until Christ be formed in you." For the true Christian must live a supernatural life in Christ: "Christ who is your life," and display it in all his actions: "That the life also of Jesus may be made manifest in our mortal flesh."
>
> For precisely this reason, Christian education takes in the whole aggregate of human life, physical and spiritual, intellectual and moral, individual, domestic and social, not with a view of reducing it in any way, but in order to elevate, regulate and perfect it, in accordance with the example and teaching of Christ.

[46] S.C.S. Off., instr., 21 mart. 1866—*Fontes,* n. 992.

[47] S.C.S. Off., instr., 24 nov. 1895—*Fontes,* n. 1046.

[48] S.C. de Prop. Fide, litt. encycl., 6 aug. 1877—*Fontes,* n. 4868; instr., 25 apr. 1868—*Fontes,* n. 4873.

> Hence the true Christian, product of Christian education, is the supernatural man who thinks, judges and acts constantly and consistently in accordance with right reason illumined by the supernatural light of the example and teaching of Christ; in other words, to use the current term, the true and finished man of character. For, it is not every kind of consistency and firmness of conduct based on subjective principles that makes true character, but only constancy in following the eternal principles of justice, as it is admitted even by the pagan poet when he praises as one and the same "the man who is just and firm of purpose." And on the other hand, there cannot be full justice except in giving to God what is due to God, as the true Christian does.[49]

The principle is clear. There can be no true education on any level unless all courses of study and all researches are made under the safe, guiding voice of the living Church of the present. To subject Catholic youth to anything short of this is dangerous, misleading, and a violation of the law of God and of His Church. It is in view of that peril to the souls of Catholic youth from non-Catholic colleges and universities that the legislator has enacted the positive prohibition. The danger is a general one, and hence the law binds all Catholic youth even though in a particular case the danger does not exist.[50]

It is within the exclusive competence of the Church to determine the matter which flows from Our Blessed Lord's commission to the Church to teach all men.[51] It is not within the province of the parents to make this determination in view of an exercise of their natural rights in the matter of the education of their children. Now, it is true that the education of the offspring is, eminently, the natural and proper right and duty of the parents from the very character of matrimony and its primary end.[52] The sound in-

---

[49] Encycl. *Divini illius Magistri—AAS,* XXII (1930), 83; The translation is from *Five Great Encyclicals* (30. printing, 1953, New York: The Paulist Press), pp. 64, 65.

[50] Can. 21.

[51] Matth. 28, 19-20.

[52] Canons 1012, § 1; 1113.

struction and adequate education of youth, however, cannot be separated from the Christian formation and the Christian education of that same youth, for there is no true education unless the youth be directed to its final end. Thus, by reason of the necessary religious and moral instruction and education, the natural right of the Church in matters of the supernatural order arises to take part in the domestic education of youth within the family circle and in that public education which is given to youth in schools.[53] When, as here, the matter is one not only of the natural order, but also, precisely, one of the supernatural order, the Church exercises a supereminent right and makes the decision as to what is useful or harmful in relation to the eternal salvation of Catholic youth.[54] For the same reasons, it is the Church, and not the student when ready for admittance to a college or a university, that renders the judgment, even though the student be emancipated from parental control in accord with the principle established in canon 89.

Article 3. The Penalties.

The supreme legislator in the Church, framing and promulgating his law for the spiritual welfare of his subjects, must be armed with coercive power as well as legislative and judicial powers if his law is to prove effectual. In the extremely important matter of the higher education of Catholic youth in universities and colleges, he must direct rational and free agents. Parents and students who can be weak or mistaken must be governed. They must respond to that government in the form of observance of the law which the legislator has promulgated. From those who would ignore the dictates of reason, the legislator seeks to secure compliance with his law with the threat of punitive and medicinal sanctions.

In the Fifth Book of the Code the legislator lists those who deliberately violate one of the prohibitions enacted in canon 1374 among the ones who are guilty of delicts against the Faith and

---

[53] Ottaviani, *Institutiones Iuris Publici Ecclesiastici*, II, 341, 343.

[54] Encycl. *Divini illius Magistri—AAS*, XXII (1930), 58.

against the Unity of the Church.[55] The wording of the canon he has included in the law to be used against them is carefully formed and requires some explanation.

It is the intention of the legislator that the most severe of ecclesiastical penalties, the censure of excommunication, be incurred by certain clases of people who deliberately entrust the formal education of Catholic youth to those who will instruct or educate[56] them in a religion which is other than the Catholic religion.[57]

The Code defines excommunication as a censure by which a person is excluded from communion with the faithful.[58] It deprives the delinquent of all participation in the common blessings of ecclesiastical society, and it entails the loss of the rights and privileges which he possesses as a member of the Church.[59] The excommunication is incurred as soon as the delinquent has perpetrated the violation and contracted the guilt, and hence he must regularly observe the penalty without delay. This rule admits of one exception under certain conditions. If the delinquent cannot observe the penalty without infamy or loss of his good name, he is not bound to do so until there has been a declaratory sentence against him.[60]

Only certain classes of people, however, are included by the legislator in this matter, namely, the actual, natural parents of the

---

[55] Pars III, Tit. XI.

[56] Here one must distinguish between instruction (*institutio*) and education (*educatio*). Instruction looks chiefly to the intellectual formation of the student, while education looks to the total formation of the spiritual faculties of the student, namely, to his intellectual, religious, moral and scientific development. Cf. Toscanel, "Annotationes ad Monitum S. Officii de associationibus communisticis puerorum," *Appollinaris* (Romae, 1928—), XXIII (1950), 266.

[57] "Subsunt excommunicationi latae sententiae Ordinario reservatae catholici parentes vel parentum locum tenentes qui liberos in religione acatholica educandos vel instituendos scienter tradunt."—Can. 2319, § 1, 4°.

[58] Can. 2257.

[59] Ayrinhac-Lydon, *Penal Legislation in the New Code of Canon Law* (rev. ed., New York, Benziger Bros., 1936), n. 111. For the specific effects of excommunication, cf. *ibid.*, nn. 115-123.

[60] Can. 2232, § 1.

student as also those who have taken the place of the parents. By these latter are meant those who actually function in the place of parents. Thus, they may be the legal guardians of the student, or older brothers or sisters, or other older relatives or friends, who make the determination of the college or university in which the student will be instructed or educated in a non-Catholic religion. For the purpose of the present study, the college or university in question must be a sectarian one or, at least, one which will have for its purpose the indoctrination of the Catholic student in a heretical belief. The Code enacts no penalties when the college or the university is a *neutral* one or one of a *mixed* character.

Further, the parents or those who take the place of the parents must be baptized Catholics and actually members of the Church, even though lax and negligent in their duties, if they are to incur the excommunication. Thus, baptized Catholics who at present are apostates, heretics or schismatics, as also baptized non-Catholics, are not subject to the penalty.[61]

Finally, perfect deliberativeness (*dolus*)[62] is postulated on the part of those who become subject to the excommunication from the use of the term *scienter* by the legislator.[63] Thus, they would have to be fully aware that the college or university in which they have placed the Catholic student is one in which such non-Catholic instruction or education is imparted, and that the Church forbids their action under pain of excommunication. The absolu-

---

[61] Cappello, *De Censuris* (Taurini, Marietti, 1925), n. 368.

[62] The Code clearly makes a distinction between *dolus* in general and the *dolus* postulated for the incurring of penalties regarding which the law has such terms as *praesumpserit, ausus fuerit,* and the like. Canon 2200, § 1, defines *dolus* as the *deliberata voluntas violandi legem,* while canon 2229, § 2, speaks of a *dolus* in which full knowledge and deliberation is necessary, and which is not had when any diminished imputability either on the side of the intellect or on the side of the will is present. Even culpable ignorance of the penalty alone suffices to bar the presence of this form of *dolus.* Cf. Swoboda, *Ignorance in Relation to the Imputability of Delicts,* The Catholic University of America Canon Law Studies, n. 143 (Washington, D. C., The Catholic University of America Press, 1941), p. 96.

[63] *Ibidem,* pp. 97, 98.

tion from the excommunication is reserved to the ordinary. Those who incur the excommunication are also suspected of hersy[64] and are subject to the penalties of canon 2315.

The Sacred Congregation of the Holy Office issued a *Monitum* on July 28, 1950,[65] concerning Communistic organizations. It is adverted to here because there are colleges and universities which are now under Communist control, following and inculcating the "party line." In the document the faithful are warned that:

(1) Parents or those who stand in their place, who contrary to canon 1372, § 2, turn their children over to the aforesaid associations to be trained, cannot be admitted to the reception of the sacraments.

(2) Those who teach boys and girls what is contrary to the faith and to Christian morals incur an excommunication specially reserved to the Holy See.

(3) The boys and girls themselves, as long as they have part in these associations, cannot be admitted to the sacraments.[66]

The Code enacts a penalty for only certain people who permit Catholic youth to be educated in a non-Catholic religion, as outlined above. This should not be taken to mean, however, that the attendance by Catholic students at colleges or universities of a neutral or of a mixed character may not be punished with ecclesiastical penalties. Canon 2220, § 1, grants coercive power to bishops for their diocese and to all other ordinaries, save the vicar-general,[67] to attach penalties to their own laws or precepts. In virtue of canon 2221, those same ordinaries may add a penal sanction to the ecclesiastical law of a higher superior which has been promulgated without such a sanction, should the circumstances in a given case warrant such action on their part. The positive ecclesiastical law prohibiting the attendance of Catholic youth at colleges and universities of a neutral or mixed character is such

[64] Can. 2319, § 2.

[65] *AAS,* XLII (1950), 553.

[66] Bouscaren, *The Canon Law Digest* (3 vols. and Supplements through 1953 and 1954, Milwaukee, Bruce & Co., 1934-1943-1953-1954-1955), III, 660, 661 (hereafter cited *Digest*).

[67] Can. 2220, § 2.

a law. It carries with it no penalty from the law enacted in the Code. If an ordinary should judge that in his diocese, or in a certain part of his diocese, the attendance of Catholic youth at a given college or university of a neutral or mixed character is preparing the way for an increasing frequency of such violations throughout the diocese, or is bringing forth abuses of one sort or another, he is empowered to enact sanctions to prevent the continuance of such attendance. In the absence of some specific penal legislation, these violations cannot ordinarily be punished as delicts. Should a particular violation, however, involve notable scandal or a special gravity, the faculty granted in canon 2222, § 1, authorizes the ordinary to treat it as a true ecclesiastical delict.[68]

---

[68] Casey, *A Study of Canon 2222, § 1,* The Catholic University of America Canon Law Studies, n. 290 (Washington, D. C., The Catholic University of America Press 1949), p. 64.

CHAPTER V

The Present Toleration

Article 1. The Nature of the Term "Toleration."

The organized and firmly entrenched errors of the Reformation and the consequent growth of private, of sectarian, of state-supported and of state-controlled universities and colleges have placed a great obstacle in the path of the Church to provide all Catholic youth with Catholic education on the higher levels. These factors and the inadequate number of Catholic universities and colleges have forced from the Church a measure of toleration which tempers the prohibition of canon 1374.[1] The actual granting of that toleration in given cases has been reserved by the legislator to local ordinaries. It is not for parents or students to take the measure, as it were, of universities or colleges of a neutral or mixed character, and then to decide the matter for themselves.

> "Solius autem Ordinarii loci est decernere, ad normam instructionum Sedis Apostolicae, in quibus rerum adiunctis et quibus adhibitis cautelis, ut periculum perversionis vitetur, tolerari possit ut eae scholae celebrentur."[2]

---

[1] In the United States, for example, there are more than 500,000 Catholics attending American universities and colleges. The 247 Catholic colleges and universities provide for fewer than 200,000 of these students. Thus, more than 60% of our Catholic college and university students are being educated in schools other than Catholic ones. These figures reflect an estimate drawn by the writer from a report made in 1953, which states: "At present there are 2.5 million students in America attending colleges and universities. About 170,000 of these attend Catholic colleges. It is safe to assume that a percentage of these are not Catholics. There are about 320,000 Catholics attending secular universities and colleges which points up the fact that approximately there are two Catholics attending secular colleges to one in Catholic colleges."—*Newman Club Manual* (The *National Newman Club Federation,* Washington, D. C., 1954), pp. 8, 9.

[2] Can. 1374.

The nature of that toleration must be carefully determined, lest it be taken for the legislator's approval or consent for the violation of his prohibition. In its general sense, toleration consists in a "forebearing disposition of soul from which flows a judgment of the mind. That judgment directs that, for serious reasons, we bear patiently those things which are opposed to and detrimental to our best interests, and hence do not meet with our approval. Finding that we are unable to prevent these things or to avoid them, or that it is not expedient to do so, we allow them to happen. Our policy, then, because of the grave reasons involved, is one of non-resistance, with no compromise of our firm disapproval."[3]

The concern of the writer here is not with the toleration between private persons, but with the toleration by which public authority patiently bears those things from its own subjects which it knows to be against its laws, when from its absolute right and power it could prohibit them. This toleration, then, is not of the weak and erroneous kind, which requires little knowledge and little will. Rather, it is presumed that the legislator knows these harmful things well. From an understanding of the matter at hand, his will is determined for the patient bearing of those things which he cannot or should not turn away from. For this reason, toleration differs from dissimulation (*dissimulatio*), since for those things about which the legislator dissimulates he feigns ignorance, and he desires that he be considered as one who is in ignorance about the matter in question. In toleration, on the other hand, he desires that it be known—he may even make it public—that he is aware of a given condition, and that it is that condition which he patiently bears or allows.

Since toleration involves things or conditions which are not for

[3] "Indulgens animi affectio indeque fluens declaratio mentis, qua ex iustis rationibus patienter ea ferimus, quae nobis adversa seu molesta sunt nobisque non probantur; quae adversa scilicet dum prohibere aut declinare vel non possumus vel non debemus, propter gravas causas, non resistendo, admittimus, quantumvis licet nostro iudicio probari nequeant."—Nilles, "Tolerari potest," in *Zeitschrift für katholische Theologie* (Innsbruck, Druck und Belang von Felicien Rauch, 1877—), XVII (1893), p. 247 (hereafter cited, "Tolerari potest").

the best interests of the community, the legislator must consider the reasons or causes for extending that toleration before he allows such things to happen. The causes which may require an act of toleration on his part can arise from three general hindrances (*impedimenta*) to a course of living in which the legislator would be free to disapprove and to reject all things which he considers to be harmful. First the hindrance may come from the civil law of the territory in which the ecclesiastical legislator functions. Thus, for example, the civil law may prohibit the establishment of a Catholic university or college, thus giving rise to a hindrance deriving from the law itself (*impedimentum legis*). Were the Catholic college in his territory levelled by a destructive storm or fire, he would be faced by a hindrance deriving from nature itself (*impedimentum naturae*), about which he is powerless. Finally, the common good may require, at least temporarily, that he exercise his power for toleration. Thus, given a Catholic university or college which is found not yet to be able, by reason of personnel or equipment or both, to offer a certain course of study, then, in such circumstances, he is faced with a hindrance occasioned by the very demand of the utility itself (*impedimentum utilitatis*).[4]

The conditions outlined above may well require the toleration spoken of in the canon, namely, the accepting as an actual fact, of those things which cannot be approved. In such instances, the ordinary may decide not to resist the attendance of Catholics at colleges and universities of a neutral or mixed character, lest some notable good for the Catholic students be jeopardized or even impaired, or lest some greater evil in the form of complete disregard and disobedience to the common law be occasioned. The Holy See has often declared that ordinaries are to follow such a procedure when they are confronted with one or more of the hindrances that can attend the project of a Catholic education.[5]

It must also be clear that when toleration is accorded it necessarily relates only to things which are harmful, odious or unpleasant, namely, to evils whether they be truly or only apparently

---

[4] *Ibidem*, p. 249.

[5] Cf. S.C. de Prop. Fide, litt. (ad Ep. Hiberniae), 16 ian. 1841—*Fontes*, n. 4787; S.C.S. Off., instr., 21 mart. 1866—*Fontes*, n. 992.

such. It is meant here that toleration is used when there is a question of moral evils or of such elements which are adverse to laws. The laws may be of two kinds: the natural law, and the positive human law. Those things which do not conform to the natural law may become the objects of toleration on the part of the legislator when he judges that a severe and hasty correction of the violations may lead to greater evils, while a patient toleration of the present violations can be borne apart from the giving of any approval for the evil. The demands of the common good may require such a judgment from him.

In matters involving the positive human law, the legislator is concerned with evils which, in consideration of the common good, are obstacles to the attainment of the end of the society. In the government of his subjects he may find that, because of error and human weakness, or because of deliberate disobedience, they have become so accustomed to odious practices that they may be diverted from them only with great difficulty, if at all. It is here that he may employ an exercise of toleration in order to avert or stave off what may be greater evils arising out of excessive rigor or from an undesirable practice of dispensing from the violated law. In practice, then, the legislator, since it is realized that all the quirks and inconsistencies of human nature cannot be encompassed and regulated by his law, is permitted to recede from the rigor of the law in such a way that the law itself need not be relaxed by means of a dispensation. In this way, the way of toleration, the legislator does not depart from his opposition to the evil practice, nor from his desire to remove it.

Toleration, in the juridic sense then, is always negative. It must be considered as existing apart from or devoid of all approval on the part of the legislator, and it abstracts from the alternative need of dispensing from the law which prohibits the harmful practice. Once conceded by the legislator, however, toleration imposes on others an obligation which prohibits them from placing anything which will impede its use within the terms of the concession.[6] Any toleration is, at best, a reluctant concession, and requires strict adherence to the terms of the concession.[7]

---

[6] Van Hove, *De Privilegiis et Dispensationibus,* n. 334.

[7] Van Hove, *De Legibus Ecclesiasticis,* n. 53, 2. Some authors liken

It has doubtless been noticed by the reader that the word "tolerance" has not been used in the preceding discussion. Its use has been deliberately avoided, for it is the opinion of the writer that tolerance conveys the idea of an attitude or a habitual state of the mind. Such an impression or concept is not the intention of the legislator. "The *"tolerari possit"* which is used in the canon by the legislator requires an investigation along the lines expressed in the canon before the ordinary is free to make any such determination. In this sense, then, the more active and the more particular meaning contained in the term "toleration" is preferred by the writer.

The basic premise in the canon, therefore, is not one of tolerance in the usual meaning of the word, which would leave the impression that the Church permits and condones the attendance of Catholics at universities and colleges of a neutral or mixed character because of existing conditions. Rather, is it to be understood that local ordinaries are to exercise a negative toleration of such an evil in keeping with the norms established in the Instructions of the Holy See. That negative toleration is to come only after a careful examination and consideration of circumstances and of the possible safeguards against the dangers to the Catholic youth in their own territory. The concession of that toleration is not to be construed as consent or approval which has replaced his opposition to the evil, or has supplanted his desire for its removal.

Toleration may be tacit or express. It is tacit when the legislator employs a deliberate and prudent silence in order to avoid greater evils. It is express in either one of two ways. When the toleration is conceded by means of a general enactment of the legislator, it is edictal (*edictalis*). If it be an express toleration

---

toleration to a permission, but they always qualify it as a *permissio comparativa,* or as one which permits that which the law does not concede, while it never grants consent or approval for that which is permitted. Cf. Michiels, *Normae Generales Iuris Canonici* (2. ed., 2 vols., Parisiis-Tournai-Romae, Desclée, 1949), II, 681 (hereafter cited *Normae Generales*); Cicognani, *Canon Law* (2. ed. revised, authorized English version by O'Hara and Brennan, Philadelphia: The Dolphin Press, 1935; reprint, Westminster, Md.: The Newman Press, 1949), p. 831; Nilles, "Tolerari potest," p. 274.

which looks to a particular case, and makes mention of the case, it is decretal (*decretalis*).[8]

Article 2. The Powers of the Local Ordinary.

In canon 198, the Code of Canon Law enumerates specifically the ecclesiastical persons who are to be considered as local ordinaries. In virtue of canon 1374, it is these who are exclusively empowered to determine the matter of toleration.[9] They are the following: the Roman Pontiff for the entire world; in their own respective territories, residential bishops, and abbots as well as prelates *nullius* together with their vicars general, administrators, vicars and prefects apostolic and the vicars delegate appointed by the vicars and prefects apostolic,[10] and finally those who by law or approved constitutions succeed the above-mentioned during a vacancy in the office or if the office is otherwise impeded, i.e., the cathedral chapter, acting as a corporate body according to canon 101,[11] the abbatial or prelatial chapter[12] before the election of a vicar capitular;[13] in mission countries, the pro-vicars and pro-

[8] Nilles, "Tolerari potest," p. 256.

[9] The published *Schema* of the Code shows that, before the promulgation of the Code, not all canonists were agreed that such power should be given to local ordinaries without previous consultation with the Holy See.—"Pueri catholici scholas acatholicas vel quae neutrae vel mixtae dicuntur, ne frequentent. Solius autem Ordinarii loci erit, *consulta prius Apostolica Sede,* decernere in quibus rerum adiunctis et quibus adhibitis cautelis, ut periculum perversionis vitetur, tolerari praedictarum scholarum frequentia possit." (Italics are the writer's). Gasparri, *Schema Codicis Iuris Canonici* (Libri I, II, (1912); III, V (1913); (1914), Romae, Typis Polyglottis Vaticanis), III, can. 657, p. 283.

[10] In a letter of the Sacred Congregation for the Propagation of the Faith dated Dec. 8, 1919, and addressed to the Vicars and Prefects Apostolic, the latter were empowered henceforth to name a vicar delegate who would have all the faculties a vicar general has by law. This was a new grant because vicars and prefects apostolic did not have, in virtue of the Code of Canon Law, the power to appoint a vicar general. Cf. *AAS,* XII (1920), 120.

[11] Can. 431.

[12] Can. 324.

[13] Can. 435.

prefects apostolic,[14] and, in countries where cathedral chapters are not constituted, the diocesan board of consultors, whose function it then becomes to designate the administrator of the vacant diocese.[15] These corporate bodies as such could make the determination of the toleration, although it seems more likely that they would wait upon the judgment of the new local ordinary in practically all cases. Religious superiors are not local ordinaries. As religious ordinaries they have jurisdiction only over their own subjects. Consequently, they are not referred to when the Code speaks of affairs in which religious in their very status as religious do not enter. The jurisdictional power of such superiors is excluded in all matters which treat of the Christian people as such. Religious superiors have no authority in legislation for the education of youth.[16]

The obvious intent of the legislator is that the toleration spoken of in canon 1374 be in the ecclesiastical jurisdiction of the local ordinary exclusively. Ecclesiastical jurisdiction comprises whatever involves the entire social power (*regimen*) of the Church.[17] As the director of good works, that is of faith and of a life according to faith, the Church exercises its social mission, while as the dispenser of grace the Church exercises its sacramental ministry. It is for the former office that the Church is endowed by Christ with jurisdiction. The power of Orders is given to the Church by Christ for the latter.[18] The actual power[19] implied in

---

[14] Can. 309, § 2.

[15] Can. 427.

[16] Can. 198, § 2; Keene, *Religious Ordinaries and Canon 198*, The Catholic University of America Canon Law Studies, n. 135 (Washington, D. C., The Catholic University of America Press, 1942), pp. 5, 6.

[17] "Iurisdictio est potestas regendi fideles in ordine ad salutem aeternam."—Prümmer, *Manuale Iuris Canonici* (4. ed., Friburgi, Herder, 1927), p. 119.

[18] Cappello, *Summa Iuris Publici Ecclesiastici* (2. ed., Romae, Apud Aedes Universitatis Gregorianae, 1929), p. 183 (hereafter cited *Summa Iuris Publici*).

[19] "Iurisdictio est potestas publica circa aliorum regimen seu gubernationem."—Reiffenstuel, *Ius Canonicum Universum*, Lib. I, tit. XXIX, n. 3.

the concept of ecclesiastical jurisdiction embraces not only disciplinary authority (*imperium*), common to all juridically perfected societies,[20] but also a doctrinal prerogative (*magisterium*), in virtue of which the Church authoritatively controls not only the behavior but also the belief of its members. This is a necessary right of the Church—this power to teach and to command assent to Christian doctrine—for it is in accordance with those doctrines that the Church formulates its disciplinary rule.

The concept of ecclesiastical jurisdiction extends not only to the relation between the individual member of the society and the society itself, as does the concept of civil jurisdiction in embracing the relationship of a citizen to his State, but ecclesiastical jurisdiction extends also to the individual's moral relation to God. Thus, the exercise of ecclesiastical jurisdiction extends to both the external and the internal forum.[21] Although the reverse is not true, a jurisdictional act of the external forum is effective in the internal forum also.[22] The matter at hand deals with the external forum directly, and thus there is no need to speak of the internal forum expressly, provided that it is clearly understood that a decision given by a confessor in the internal forum may well abolish a previous concession of toleration granted to a Catholic student for attending a college or a university of a neutral or mixed character.

It remains now to examine the personnel in the Church to

---

[20] Man as a social being has a double destiny, a temporal and an eternal happiness. In the present divine economy, no one society is ordained to satisfy both the natural and the supernatural demands of human nature. The State and the Church, then, distinguished by the purposes they pursue, are juridically perfected societies in that they tend to the total perfection of their own order and have a native right to all the means necessary to pursue their distinct ends. The State in each of its territorial and national divisions and the One Universal Church are the two distinct, juridically perfected societies. Cf. Leo XIII, ep. encycl., *Immortale Dei,* 1 nov. 1885 —*Fontes,* n. 592; Ottaviani, *Institutiones Iuris Publici Ecclesiastici,* I, nn. 21, 25, 33.

[21] Can. 196; "Ad forum externum pertinent actiones quibus fideles in facie Ecclesiae iusti aut rei fiunt, ad internum actiones qua iusti aut rei sunt coram Deo."—Vermeersch-Creusen, *Epitome,* I, n. 313.

[22] Can. 202, § 1.

whom ecclesiastical jurisdiction is entrusted. From the Will of its Founder, Jesus Christ, the official power of the Church, both sacramental and jurisdictional or social, is radically invested in one person, the pope. He may be considered an absolute monarch in one sense, and in another sense as a constitutional monarch. He is an absolute monarch in the sense that his supreme, spiritual power cannot be vetoed by any other authority on earth inside or outside the Church. In virtue of the constitution of the Church as established by Christ, although the pope is supreme, he is not the sole authority.[23] The power of the Church is not isolated and confined only to his person. It is also vested in the body of the clergy, those set apart under him by Christ to teach, govern and minister to the faithful.[24] The clergy, moreover, while distinct from the body of the faithful, as superiors from their subjects, are hierarchically distinguished among themselves.[25]

The power of jurisdiction of the residential bishop[26] is ordinary because it is inherent in the office,[27] but the office itself is subordinate. The subordinate nature of the episcopal office follows from the jurisdictional primacy of the Sovereign Pontiff as defined in the Vatican Council.[28] The limitations of the subordinate

---

[23] "Si Petri eiusque successorum plena ac summa potestas est, ea tamen esse ne putetur sola."—Leo XIII, ep. encycl., *Satis cognitum,* 29 iunii, 1896 —*Fontes,* n. 630.

[24] Can. 107; Conc. Trident., sessio XXIII, *de ordine,* c. 4—Schroeder, pp. 161, 162.

[25] Can. 108, § 2. By hierarchy (sacred government) is meant the ministers or officials of the Church arranged according to the degree of spiritual power or authority which they possess.—Coronata, *Institutiones,* I, n. 167. This distinction is applicable to the power of orders as well as to the power of jurisdiction. These powers are distinct, and they differ principally by reason of their immediate origin and purpose. The one is directly conferred by way of ordination, the other by way of canonical mission. The one is directly intended for the individual, the other for the social benefit.—Cappello, *Summa Iuris Publici,* pp. 183-187.

[26] The writer limits himself to a discussion of the residential bishop's jurisdiction. By reason of office and canonical mission, all those enumerated in canon 198 as local ordinaries enjoy the same jurisdiction in the matters which are regulated by canon 1374, even though not all local ordinaries are always bishops with powers of the episcopal order.

[27] Canons 197, § 1; 334, § 1.

[28] "Docemus proinde et declaramus, Ecclesiam Romanam, disponente

episcopal office are extrinsic, that is, it is intended for the government of a diocese only,[29] and intrinsic from the limitations which the nature of the Primacy imposes on the nature of the Episcopacy. The plenitude and universality of the papal jurisdiction characterize the ordinary power of the residential bishop as fundamentally limited, whereas the supreme and immediate jurisdiction of the pope renders the jurisdiction of the residential bishop as a power which may be limited in its functions.[30]

The limitations on the power of the local ordinary for the granting of the toleration mentioned in canon 1374 are in the form of guidance from the supreme legislator, but the local ordinary must be guided by the Instructions of the Holy See in his judgment and in his regulations as the canon indicates. The actual application of the norms of those Instructions of the Holy See is given over to the immediate judgment of the local ordinary, since the supreme legislator is fully aware of the fact that conditions, attitudes and circumstances will vary from diocese to diocese or even within a single diocese.

Only baptized Catholics are the subjects regulated by the law contained in canon 1374, provided, or course, that they are in the process of acquiring a formal education.[31] These baptized Cath-

---

Domino, super omnes alias ordinariae potestatis obtinere principatum, et hanc Romani Pontificis iurisdictionis potestatem, quae vere episcopalis est, immediatam esse: erga quam cuiuscunque ritus et dignitatis pastores atque fideles, tam seorsum singuli quam simul omnes, officio hierarchicae subordinationis veraeque oboedientiae obstringuntur, non solum in rebus, quae ad fidem et mores, sed etiam in iis, quae ad disciplinam et regimen Ecclesiae per totum orbem diffusae pertinent; ita ut, custodita cum Romano Pontifice tam communionis quam fidei professionis unitate, Ecclesia Christi sit unus grex sub uno summo pastore. Haec est catholicae veritatis doctrina, a qua deviare salva fide atque salute nemo potest."—Denzinger, *Enchiridion Symbolorum,* n. 1827.

29 Can. 334, § 1.

30 Canons 108, § 3; 329. Thus, the theory advanced in the Synod of Pistoia to the effect that the bishop receives from Christ all rights necessary for the government of his diocese, and that therefore no higher competent authority is required, was condemned.—Pius VI, const., *Auctorem fidei,* 17 aug. 1794—*Fontes,* n. 475.

31 Can. 12.

olics become the subjects of a particular local ordinary if they have a domicile[32] or a quasi-domicile[33] in his territory and are actually residing there.[34] The inclusion of Catholic strangers or travelers (*peregrini*) among those who are bound by the determinations of the local ordinary in the matter of attendance at a college or a university of a neutral or mixed character requires some explanation.

Section 1. *Peregrini.*

The common English word used by commentators in designation of a *peregrinus* is "stranger."[35] In Canon Law, a "stranger" is a person who has a domicile or a quasi-domicile, but is not actually in the territory of either.[36] Catholic students, if they are minors, will have either the domicile or the quasi-domicile of their parents unless they have acquired their own quasi-domicile.[37] Having reached their majority, i.e., having completed their twenty-first year,[38] Catholic students may have their own domicile or quasi-domicile. When Catholic students seek to attend a college or a

[32] Domicile is acquired, under the Code of Canon Law, in consequence either of intention and residence, or of residence alone for a period of ten years in a parish or, at least, in a diocese.—Can. 92, § 1.

[33] Quasi-domicile is acquired in consequence either of residence in a place with the intention of remaining there for the greater part of the year, or of actual residence, even apart from the element of intention, for the greater part of the year.—Can. 92, § 2.

[34] Can. 13, § 2.

[35] Cf. Augustine, *A Commentary on the New Code of Canon Law* (8 vols., Vol. I, 5. ed., St. Louis, Herder & Co., 1926), I, 27 (hereafter cited *Commentary*); Cicognani, *Canon Law,* p. 578; Bouscaren-Ellis, *Canon Law,* p. 27; Woywod-Smith, *A Practical Commentary on the Code of Canon Law* (rev. ed., 2 vols., New York, J. F. Wagner, Inc., 1948), I, 8 (hereafter cited *Commentary*). Hammill (1913-1949) used the word "traveler" when speaking of a *peregrinus* in his work, *The Obligations of the Traveler According to Canon 14,* The Catholic University of America Canon Law Studies, n. 160 (Washington, D. C.: The Catholic University of America Press, 1942), p. 1 (hereafter cited *The Obligations of the Traveler*).

[36] Can. 91.

[37] Can. 93, § 2.

[38] Can. 88, § 1.

university of a neutral or mixed character in a territory in which they have a parochial or a diocesan domicile or, at least, a diocesan quasi-domicile, they are subject to the ordinary of that diocese in the matter of securing the toleration spoken of in canon 1374. In the same way, Catholic students, when they petition the ordinary's toleration for their attendance at a college or a university of a neutral or mixed character at which they will be boarding-students, make their application to the ordinary of the diocese in which the school is located, in virtue of the acquisition there of a quasi-domicile.[39]

There seems to be a difficulty when one considers the legal position of Catholic students who seek to attend a college or a university of a neutral or mixed character in a diocese other than the one in which they maintain a domicile or a quasi-domicile, when they will be merely day-students at the college or the university in question. In such circumstances they hold the position of the "strangers" spoken of in canon 14, inasmuch as they do not acquire a domicile or a quasi-domicile for the reason that there is lacking the essential element of residence.[40] For the pur-

[39] Such students simply by their residence, when it is personal, morally continuous, and computed according to canon 34, § 3, 1° and 3°, acquire a quasi-domicile, provided the residence has continued for the greater part of the year. In these circumstances a quasi-domicile is acquired, even though the intention of the students be to the contrary. "It is quite generally agreed that week-end absence, even though repeated each week, as in the case of students and teachers, would not destroy the continuity."—Costello, *Domicile and Quasi-Domicile,* The Catholic University of America Canon Law Studies, n. 60 (Washington, D. C.: The Catholic University of America, 1930), pp. 140, 141.

[40] "This element consists in actual dwelling in the place; a personal, physical presence in a place *per modum inhabitantis.* The residence must be personal. It is enough that one buy or possess a home in a certain place; neither is it enough that one transfer a greater part of his belongings to a place. Merely material occupancy of this character does not suffice. The word *commoratio* denotes a personal, physical presence. The residence must be *per modum inhabitantis.* It seems that to dwell in a place after the manner of an inhabitant, it is not enough to spend the hours of the day there. One must live there, spend the night there, have his hearth-stone there (*lares*), however meager and barren that may be." —Costello, *op. cit.,* pp. 116-119.

pose of this work, the term "traveler," as employed by Hammill, seems preferable to the writer when one considers that the Catholic students described seek to become, in our modern parlance, commuters to and from a particular college or university.

The provisions of canon 1374 make it obvious that the local ordinary is to particularize the law of the Code[41] for his subjects in the matter of attendance at colleges or universities of a neutral or mixed character within the confines of his diocese. It is the subjection to or the freedom from these particular laws of the local ordinary on the part of the one who would become a traveler by reason of his seeking to pursue his education in such a college or university that must be determined. Canon 14, § 1, 2°, states the principles governing the obligation of a traveler to observe the particular laws that obtain in the place of his daily sojourning.[42]

Although canon 14, § 1, 2°, does not explicity mention particular laws, it evidently refers only to particular laws. The text of this part of the canon concerns the "laws of the territory." This

[41] "Exceptionaliter tamen quaedam leges particulares pro peculiari territorio conditae *absolute seu plenius territoriales sunt,* ita ut attingant *omnes qui et quamdiu de facto seu actu commorantur in territorio isto,* non exclusis peregrinis et vagis nullam sedem juridicam stabilem in territorio isto habentibus.

a) Obvium est *ex se* nihil obstare, quominus de facto tales condantur leges, non solummodo a legislatore supremo, cujus 'potestas est vere episcopalis, ordinaria et immediata tum in omnes et singulas ecclesias, tum in omnes et singulos pastores et fideles' (can. 218, § 2), sed etiamvero a legislatoribus particularibus, quorum potestas legislativa restringitur ad territorium determinatum; ipsis sane ex se talis et tanta agnoscenda est et de facto a legislatore supremo agnoscitur potestas legislativa, qualis et quanta necessaria est ad apte promovendum et secure protegendum bonum commune territorii eorum curae concrediti, seu rectius, communitatis fidelium in eorum territorio stabilem sedem habentium; jamvero promotio et protectio istius boni communis exigere potest, ut in quibusdam circumstantiis vel relate ad quasdam materias eorum legibus non solummodo subjiciantur incolae et advenae, ad quorum salutem directe ordinantur istae leges, sed et extranei hic et nunc in eorum territorio versantes." Michiels, *Normae Generales,* I, 389, 390.

[42] Peregrini "neque legibus territorii in quo versantur [tenentur], iis exceptis quae ordini publico consulunt, vel actuum sollemnia determinant."

phrase interpreted by canon 13, § 2,[43] refers to those laws which are enacted for a definite territory. Furthermore, canon 14, § 1, 3°, states the discipline regarding the universal laws in force in a particular territory. This reference would hardly be necessary if the previous paragraph had reference to universal laws as well as to particular laws. Hence, canon 14, § 1, 2°, refers to particular laws and only to particular laws.

Now the formal object of all ecclesiastical jurisdiction, and of legislative jurisdiction in particular, is a personal object, the government of subjects for the sanctification of their souls.[44] Subjection to the authority in a society is derived from membership in that society by reason of some title. In a particular society whose medium of jurisdiction is territorial, this membership is naturally derived from a local association or bond.[45] Since membership in a society implies a mutual activity of all of the members for a common objective, the membership in the society is more complete as this local association is more fixed and stable.[46] The care of those who have a fixed residence in the territory is the primary and principal purpose of the institution of a particular legislative authority in the Church.[47] Travelers, then, who have a fixed residence elsewhere, remain essentially and virtually subject to the local legislator of their place of residence, and the ordinary title of jurisdiction over them belongs to that legislator, and not to the legislator in whose territory they are travelers. Therefore, the legislator of the place of the college or the university they desire to attend cannot, ordinarily, oblige them to observe his laws.[48]

There are, however, certain extraordinary titles by which these travelers are subject to the laws of the particular legislator in

---

[43] "Legibus conditis pro peculiari territorio ii subiiciuntur pro quibus latae sunt quique ibidem domicilium vel quasi-domicilium habent et simul actu commorantur, firmo praescripto can. 14."

[44] Ottaviani, *Institutiones Iuris Publici Ecclesiastici*, I, nn. 113, 117.

[45] Wernz-Vical, *Ius Canonicum*, I, n. 147, note 99.

[46] Ottaviani, *Institutiones Iuris Publici Ecclesiastici*, I, n. 17.

[47] Ryan, *Principles of Episcopal Jurisdiction*, The Catholic University of America Canon Law Studies, n. 120 (Washington, D. C., The Catholic University of America Press, 1939), pp. 100-101.

[48] Hammill, *The Obligations of the Traveler*, p. 120.

whose territory the college or the university of a neutral or mixed character is located. The presence and the conduct of travelers may affect the welfare of the ordinary subjects of a local ordinary, and they must be subject at such times to the government of the local ordinary.[49]

The title of authority over baptized Catholic travelers in the matter of their attendance at colleges or universities of a neutral or mixed character is a threefold one in virtue of canon 1374. The prohibition arises from the natural law, the import and content of which has been clarified in the universal law of the Church. The supreme legislator has expressly conceded the particular application of the law to the legislative power of the local ordinaries, who are to make the specific determinations under which all those in their territories may consider themselves free to avail themselves of the toleration which may have been conceded, or hold themselves prohibited from attendance at a particular college or university.

It must be established, however, that the particular laws of the local legislator are laws which secure the public order in his territory, for such is the requirement of the Code,[50] before the traveler can be obliged to the observance of his particular laws.

Although the Code uses the term "public order" in canon 14 only, it speaks of the "public good' in several places. The choice of the term by the supreme legislator makes it clear that he sought to indicate that the particular laws of a local ordinary must contain the characteristic of securing the public order in his territory, and not the public good alone, before they oblige travelers. The exact notion of the juridical concept of "public order" is not a matter of agreement among commentators. The mind of the legislator is certainly to be interpreted that he wanted an exactness

[49] "In his function as guardian of the spiritual welfare and public good of all the ordinary and complete subjects of his particular territory, the local legislator requires all the power necessary to maintain that welfare unimpaired. Therefore there are certain extraordinary and exceptional titles of subjection to the jurisdiction of the local legislator, namely, indirect subjection, the natural law, universal law, civil law, and public order."—Hammill, *op. cit.*, pp. 120, 121.

[50] ". . . quae ordini publico consulunt . . ."—Can. 14, § 1, 2°.

which would distinguish "public order" from "public good." Hammill's description that "the juridical concept of public order in the Church may be described as that strict uniformity of conduct on the part of everyone in the community, which is indispensable for the good organization of ecclesiastical society, or which is required in order that the individual members of the society may attain their personal sanctification unhindered by the actions of those around them,"[51] places the distinction between the public order and the public good in the fact that, although the terms are generically the same, they are not co-extensive. The public good pertains to whatever tends to further the welfare of the community, or to whatever is of interest to all the members of the community. It does not, however, invariably imply the note of social necessity, but applies equally well to what is to the common advantage of all, without being in any sense indispensable.[52] The two elements essentially inherent in the concept of the public order are public necessity and a strict uniformity of conduct on the part of everyone in the territory as requisite for the demands made by that public necessity.

The principles of the public order are based on the divine law and the universal canon law. There can be no thought of a public order that contradicts these principles. It is very often the function of particular laws to determine the essential public order of the

---

[51] *The Obligations of the Traveler,* n. 7 of his *Conclusions* following p. 172.

[52] Van Hove, *De Legibus,* n. 216; "Tales [leges ordini publico consulentes] dicendae sunt eae solae, sed omnes (sive prohibitivae seu praeventivae, sive etiam praeceptivae seu actum positivum exigentes), *quae ex ipso suo scopo* directe ad hoc tendunt seu praecise ad hunc finem immediatum latae sunt ut apte muniatur et secure protegatur *ordo* publicus ad bonum publicum communitatis determinatae de qua agitur prorsus necessarius, quarumque reverentia seu *observantia effectiva* in territorio igitur ad ordinem publicum assecurandum adeo *necessaria* est, ut ex *qualibet* earum violatione, a *qualibet* persona in territorio versante percata, securitas publica totius communitatis de facto vel saltem ex praesumptione periculi communis in discrimen vocatur seu communitas tota damnum patitur."—Michiels, *Normae Generales,* I, 392, 393; Cf. Cappello, *Summa Iuris Publici,* I, n. 80; Beste, *Introductio in Codicem* (3. ed., Collegeville, Minn.: St. John's Abbey Press, 1946), p. 72.

Church as it is applied to the accidentals of time and place, or to secure the public order of the particular ecclesiastical society.[53] For this reason, the Code states that particular laws which secure the public order are to be observed by travelers in the territory.

Accordingly, when a local ordinary, after a careful consideration of the circumstances existing in his territory, determines that a certain procedure is to be followed by his subjects in the matter of securing the toleration for attendance at colleges or universities of a neutral or mixed character in his territory, his particular law is to be observed by travelers also. That law would be among the minimum requirements for the good organization of his territory, requiring uniformity of conduct in a matter included in the universal law of the Church. Such a law can be identified by the clear statement of the text of the law itself, by an authentic interpretation given by the legislator, or by an investigation of the particular traveler himself.[54] In the absence of a clear statement in the text of the law that is designed to secure the public order, the stranger must seriously examine whether or not the statute can be reasonably considered as a law for regulating the public order. Once he has exercised due care to identify these laws, his judgment whether he is obliged to observe the law or not prevails until an authentic interpretation is given.[55] A clear statement indicating that a given law means to secure the public order is greatly to be desired. Examples of expressions which will give such indications can be found in canons 290, § 1; 301, § 2; 343, § 1, and 1320. It is suggested that such an expression be always included in the particular law which seeks to secure the public order. Thus there can be avoided the misconceptions which would serve to disrupt the desired uniformity of conduct.

---

[53] Van Hove, *De Legibus,* n. 216.

[54] Cf. Roelker, "The Traveler and Local Statutes," *The Jurist* (The School of Canon Law, The Catholic University of America, 1941—), II (1942), 110-115.

[55] *Loc. cit.*

Section 2. Clerics and Women Religious.

The care to be exercised by the local ordinary in the matter of clerics and men religious attending colleges and universities of a neutral or mixed character has been the object of several documents emanating from the Holy See. The first of these was an Instruction from the Sacred Congregation of Bishops and Regulars in 1896,[56] addressed to the Bishops and to the Superiors of Religious Orders and Congregations in Italy. It ordered that no secular cleric was to attend a secular university without the express permission of his bishop. The bishop was to grant that permission only when the degree to be obtained by the cleric was required in order that the bishop's schools be staffed with approved teachers. Those Orders and Congregations which were not engaged in teaching in the schools were not to send any students to the secular universities. A novice was never to be given this permission, even though he was a member of a teaching Order or Congregation. The Superior-General could extend the permission to professed clerics only when the needs of the colleges and the schools of his Order or Congregation required such a concession. Pope St. Pius X made these particular prescriptions universal in his encyclical letter *Pascendi,* of September 7, 1907, [57] and repeated his instructions in 1910.[58]

It seems that clerics had begun to attend secular universities in some appreciable numbers, and without the permission of their ordinaries, for in 1918, less than a month after the new Code of Canon Law had become the common law, the Sacred Consistorial Congregation issued a Decree[59] which confirmed the previous dispositions of the Holy See. In answer to the requests of some ordinaries who had found that the practice of attending secular

---

[56] S.C. Ep. et Reg., instr., 21 iul. 1896—*Fontes,* n. 2031.

[57] "Quae de celebrandis universitatibus sacrum Consilium Episcoporum et Religiosorum negotiis praepositum clericis Italiae tum saecularibus tum regularibus praecepit anno 1896, ea ad nationes omnes posthac pertinere decernimus."—*Fontes,* n. 680.

[58] S. Pius X, motu proprio, *Sacrorum Antistitum,* 1 sept. 1910—*Fontes,* n. 689.

[59] S.C. Consist., decr., 1 iun. 1918, *AAS,* X (1918), 237.

universities had served to weaken the faith of some of their clerics, the Sacred Congregation, at the injunction of Pope Benedict XV, decreed:

1. No cleric is to be sent to a secular university unless he is already ordained to the priesthood, and unless he be one who gives promise of being a credit to the ecclesiastical order both by the force and perspicacity of his mind and by his holiness of life.

2. In sending any of his priests to secular universities, a Bishop should have no other purpose than the need or advantage of his diocese, namely to provide suitable teachers for its schools.

3. Priests so attending secular universities are not thereby exempt from the examinations which are prescribed in canons 130 and 590; on the contrary, they should be the more strictly required to undergo them, lest through interest in profane sciences they neglect ecclesiastical studies, contrary to the prescriptions of canon 129.

4. After finishing their studies in any secular university, the priests remain subject to their ordinary in exactly the same way as before, and they remain bound to the service of the diocese. Hence, no one of them has the right to accept at will a professorship or other office, especially against the wishes of his ordinary. If anyone does so, let him be punished with suitable penalties, not excluding suspension.

5. All of this applies, *congrua congruis referendo,* to religious, and even to regulars.[60]

Only a priest may be given permission to attend universities which are not Catholic, and the permission is to be granted by the ordinary only when the needs of the diocese require such study. Every non-exempt priest religious is required to have the express permission of his local ordinary before he may attend any secular university, whether that university be of a neutral or of a mixed character. An exempt priest religious must have the express permission of the major superior who is designated by the Code as the ordinary of such a priest.[61] As a point of law, a

[60] Translation from Bouscaren; *Digest,* I, 115.

[61] The major or higher superiors are the Abbot Primate the Abbot Superior of a monastic Congregation, the Abbot of an independent (*sui iuris*)

discussion may be instituted concerning the necessity of an exempt priest religious securing the express permission of the local ordinary to attend a secular university after having secured the express permission of his major superior. Ellis holds that no such additional permission is required.[62] The exemption which canon 615[63] grants seems to confirm his position. Is the same conclusion valid when an exempt priest religious seeks to attend a secular university in the territory of a diocese other than the one in which his monastery (*domus*) is located? Commentators maintain that the single, express permission of his major superior would suffice in such an instance, since canon 1374 is not to be listed among the canons which furnish exceptions to the general rule of exemption granted in canon 615.[64] The rare possibility which makes an exempt priest religious subject to an ordinary other than his major superior arises when the local ordinary of the territory which contains a secular university requires that everyone seeking to attend the university secure his express permission for reasons of public order. In such circumstances, even though the exempt priest religious is not bound by reason of his being a traveler (*peregrinus*) pursuing a summer course of two or three months' duration,[65] he would be bound to seek the express permission of the local ordinary for the sake of the common good, although his

---

monastery, even though it forms part of a monastic Congregation, the Superior-General of the entire Institute, the Provincial Superior, their vicars and all others who have powers equal to those of Provincials.—Can. 488, 8°. Major superiors in clerical, exempt Institutes have ecclesiastical jurisdiction in both the internal and the external forum over their subjects. —Can. 501, § 1.

[62] *Periodica,* XXVII (1938), 107, 108.

[63] Regulars, both men and women, including novices, except those nuns who are not subject to regular superiors, are exempt, together with their houses and churches, from the jurisdiction of the local ordinary, except in the cases provided for by law.

[64] Vermeersch-Creusen, *Epitome,* I, n. 715; Bouscaren-Ellis, *Canon Law, pp.* 292, 293, 294.

[65] Canon 615 exempts all regulars and where the law does not distinguish, an interpreter may not distinguish.—*Corpus Iuris Civilis* (3 vols., Vol. I, *Institutiones,* quae recognovit P. Krueger; *Digesta,* quae recognovit T. Mommsen et retractavit P. Krueger, Berolini: Apud Weidmannos, 1928), D. (32. 25).

obligation would arise only indirectly, and not strictly from the positive ecclesiastical law.[66]

A difficulty which has a close relationship to the matter discussed above was presented to the Holy See in 1920. It was presented by some of the bishops of Italy. It had become a frequent practice for zealous, young priests to seek permission from their bishops to attend Normal Schools, so that they might become qualified under the civil law to teach in the public, elementary schools in Italy. The solution of the Holy See is contained in a letter from Cardinal Gasparri, the Secretary of State for Pope Benedict XV.[67] Pope Pius XI ratified and confirmed the provisions of the Circular Letter and ordered that they be made public for all ordinaries in 1927.[68] The Circular had provided:

1. Ordinaries are to permit clerics to study in normal schools only after having finished the seminary studies and having been ordained to the priesthood.

2. They are to forbid absolutely attendance at mixed schools, i.e., which are attended also by girls. They are also to designate the place where such studies are pursued, and to select those where the danger is lessened by ecclesiastical vigilance.

3. If away from home, the priest is to stay in an ecclesiastical institution, or at a priest's house.

4. If outside his diocese, he is to be under the vigilance of the ordinary of the place, who shall report to his ordinary.

---

[66] Nihilominus personae ecclesiasticae *exemptae,* v.g. regulares, quae non sunt *de territorio,* praeter casus in iure expressos saepe non directe et stricto iure, tamen indirecte propter bonum commune et scandalum vitandum tenentur ad observandas leges Episcoporum vel Synodorum particularium."—Wernz-Vidal, *Ius Canonicum,* I (2. ed., 1952), n. 149; Cf. c. 16, 17, X, *de excessibus praelatorum et subditorum,* V, 31.

[67] The letter was never published in the *Acta Apostolicae Sedis,* but it does appear in *Periodica,* XVI (1927), 61-65, as having been issued on November 18, 1920.

[68] "The prescriptions of the Holy See regarding clerics and priests who are attending Universities or so-called Normal Schools remain in effect; especially those which are contained in a letter of the Secretary of State, of Nov. 20, 1920, are to be observed exactly."—S.C. Conc., decr., 22 febr. 1927—*AAS,* XIX (1927), 99.

5. After finishing his studies, the priest remains assigned to the service of his diocese and subject to his bishop; cannot take a position as a teacher without his consent; and this consent is revocable. The bishop should try to employ him as a teacher in his diocese; but may permit him temporarily to go elsewhere to teach; but may also afterward recall him to work in the diocese; and the priest must obey without excuse.

6. These norms are retroactive, i.e., they apply to priests already studying in normal schools, or teaching.

7. Before permitting any of his priests to study in normal schools or to teach in public schools, the bishop is to show the priest these regulations, and have him subscribe to them, and also warn him that they are to be obeyed under ecclesiastical sanctions.

These regulations are sent at the request of His Holiness.[69]

Only priests, then, are to be granted a toleration for attendance at universities of a neutral or mixed character or at Normal Schools, and the legislator has imposed explicit conditions which are to be observed carefully and exactly.[70] It must be remembered that, when it is said that the toleration is to be extended only to priests, an exception exists when an Order or an Institute possesses a privilege.[71]

---

[69] Translation from Bouscaren; *Digest,* I, 118, 119.

[70] An Instruction containing a number of *Normae* from the Sacred Congregation of Seminaries and Universities, issued on August 20, 1942, makes it incumbent upon ordinaries to secure a *Nihil obstat* from the Sacred Congregation before they may grant permission for priests, secular or religious, or for women religious to attend civil universities. The Instruction has not appeared in the *Acta Apostolicae Sedis.* It can be found in the *Commentarium pro Religiosis et Missionariis* (Romae, 1920—), XXIV (1943), 3-6. Tabera in his *Annotationes* in the same volume (p. 8) says that he does not know whether the document was sent to the Ordinaries of Italy only, or to all the ordinaries in the Church. Bouscaren makes of it a document which contains norms for Italy only.—*Digest,* III, 63.

[71] Tabera cites a privilege of the Salesians in this matter: "Rector Maior, onerata conscientia, indulgere potest ut, in casu verae necessitatis, *etiam qui nondum sacerdotio sunt insigniti,* Universitates laicas ad gradus academicos consequendos frequentent, dummodo certo absit periculum

In the consideration of women religious, the Code distinguishes between those who take solemn vows and those who take simple vows. Those who take solemn vows, nuns (*moniales*) in the strict sense, and who by reason of their Constitutions depend on the jurisdiction of regular superiors, are subject to the local ordinary in those cases only which are expressly defined in the law of the Code.[72] Such Orders of women would be exempt from the jurisdiction of the local ordinary in the same manner as the exempt priests religious spoken of above. This general legislation, however, is determined by special law which, while it concedes that women religious who take solmen vows are nuns, requires that they be subject, nevertheless, to the jurisdiction of the local ordinary rather than to the jurisdiction of a regular superior.[73] Thus, in France, Belgium and the United States of America, nuns do not enjoy any exemption in regard to the local ordinaries and are not subject to the superiors of regular Orders.[74] Only an Apostolic Indult could provide such nuns with exemption in the strict sense. All other women religious take simple vows, temporary or perpetual, and the religious institutes of which they are members, are designated by the Code as Congregations.[75] A Congregation of women may never be subjected to a religious Order or Congregation of men, unless a special indult is granted to that effect. Nor is any Order or Congregation of men permitted to retain the care and direction of such Sisters, as if they were especially entrusted to them.[76] No religious institution of men, be it exempt or non-exempt may claim any jurisdiction or authority over any women religious unless such has been granted to them by the Holy See. As non-exempt religious, all women religious,

---

damni spiritualis et subditi ingenio et virtute praefulgeant."—*Commentarium pro Religiosis et Missionariis,* XXIV (1943), 16.

[72] Can. 500, § 2.

[73] Can. 488, 7°; Cf. Coronata, *Institutiones,* I, n. 530.

[74] S.C. de Relig., 22 maii, 1919—*AAS,* XI (1919), 240; S.C. de Relig., 23 iunii, 1923—*AAS,* XV (1923), 257. Cf. Creusen, *Religious Men and Women in the Code* (5. ed., revised and edited by A. C. Ellis, Milwaukee, Bruce Publishing Co., 1953), n. 53.

[75] Can. 488, 2°.

[76] Can. 500, § 3.

unless an indult makes other provision, are subject to the jurisdiction of the local ordinary in the matter of attendance at colleges or universities of a neutral or mixed character. In the light of canon 490 of the Code, the toleration of the local ordinary in the case of women religious must follow the norms established by the Holy See for clerics and men religious. Certainly, the dangers from such attendance would be as great, if not greater, for women religious than they are for priests who are trained for long periods in spiritual things and the sacred sciences, and the solicitude of the legislator for the spiritual welfare of women religious is no less earnest and real than it is for that of men religious.[77]

Section 3. Vigilance and Visitation.

The powers of the local ordinary in matters of the education which is imparted in universities and colleges are part of the doctrinal prerogative (*magisterium*) of the Church.[78] His jurisdiction in these matters comes as a result of his office and of his canonical mission[79] in the Church to which Jesus Christ has entrusted the Deposit of Faith.[80] The obligations of the hierarchy as legislators for given territories are concerned with the diffusion, conservation and defense of all the truths contained in the Deposit of Faith. It follows, then, that the furtherance of truth and the suppression

---

[77] "Quae de religiosis statuuntur, etsi masculino vocabulo expressa, valent etiam pari iure de mulieribus, nisi ex contextu sermonis vel ex rei natura aliud constet."—Can. 490.

[78] The object of that ecclesiastical *magisterium* embraces the truths of faith, the doctrines connected with those truths, and the errors which are in opposition to the truths of faith or which produce the danger of losing the faith. That magisterium is exercised in three ways, i.e., through the authentic definitions of the Church, the preaching of the word of God, and the imparting of Christian truths in schools. Cf. Wernz-Vidal, *Ius Canonicum,* IV, nn. 617, 664.

[79] "Missio canonica est *positiva* designatio ab auctoritate ecclesiastica facta ad docendam religionem Christianam."—Wernz-Vidal, *Ius Canonicum,* IV, n. 633.

[80] "Christus Dominus fidei depositum Ecclesiae concredidit, ut ipsa, Spiritu Sancto iugiter assistente, doctrinam revelatam sancte custodiret et fideliter exponeret."—Can. 1322, § 1.

"Ecclesiae, independenter a qualibet civili potestate, ius est et officium

of error must engage their attention and their vigilance. As one holding the primacy of ecclesiastical jurisdiction, the obligation of vigilance devolves upon the pope, radically and primarily. As one in the hierarchy holding, by way of subordination, an ecclesiastical office second only to that of the pope in ecclesiastical jurisdiction, the local ordinary is to exercise vigilance over universities and colleges in the measure that has been imposed upon him by the supreme legislator in the Church.[81]

The Code repeats that it is the province of the Church to inspect and to regulate the religious instruction of youth in all schools.[82] This is the basic truth and prerogative which has suffered from the gradual and determined violations of the State and civil authorities because of an erroneous conception of the spheres of influence and of jurisdiction in the two societies, the Church and the State.[83] In order that no religious error or danger to Christian

---

gentes omnes evangelicam doctrinam docendi: hanc vero rite ediscere veramque Dei Ecclesiam amplecti omnes divina lege tenentur."—Can. 1322, § 2.

[81] Cf. *supra,* pp. 96, 97; cans. 108, §§ 2, 3; 329, § 1.

[82] "Religiosa iuventutis institutio in scholis quibuslibet auctoritati et inspectioni Ecclesiae subiicitur."—Can. 1381, § 1.

[83] Boffa states it very clearly when he says: "The authoritative supervision of religion, when taught in the school, must fall entirely within the competence of the Church. This is true irrespective of the necessity of teaching religion in the school either as a mere subject on the curriculum, or as a vital educative element. To deny this is tantamount to implying that the Church lacks that exclusive juridical power which, as a divinely established society she has in the field of religion and morals. It is equivalent to setting up either the individual or the State as the sole agent in matters of faith and morality. The Church by her very nature is a juridical person. She is supreme in the spiritual sphere, and empowered with all the means necessary for the exercise and performance of her mission.

Individuals and families, as members of the Church by baptism, must conform to her directions concerning the religious education of their children. The State, as promoter of the rights and duties of families, must abide by whatever the Church ordains in what constitutes her sphere of jurisdiction. To attribute to the State any control over matters touching directly the spiritual order, as for instance, the religious training of youth, would be to confuse the spheres of the two societies. Religious training, both as a subject to be taught and as a vital educative element, pertains

morals creep into the education and into the associations of Catholic youth in universities and colleges, the Code requires that the local ordinary exercise a careful watchfulness over all the universities and colleges in his territory. In canon 1381, § 2, the Code terms that supervision "the right and duty of vigilance,"[84] and extends it to the right of approval or rejection of books and teachers of religion used in the universities and colleges, and the right of removal of the books and the teachers if they offend against faith and morals.[85] There is yet another canonical requirement to be fulfilled by the local ordinary with regard to universities and colleges. He is to "visit" those in his territory in order to determine the nature and the content of the religious and moral training being given to the students.[86] The local ordinary has a twofold right and obligation: that of vigilance and that of visitation. The right of vigilance and visitation, as the terms are used in the Code, are not the same. The right of vigilance does not include the right of visitation. While they are not the same, they are very similar and the precise distinction between them is not easy to define. Both rights imply some measure of jurisdiction; a person or a place may be subject to vigilance or to visitation, although in a general sense such a person or place may be exempt.[87]

The general definition of a canonical visitation[88] which is the

---

by divine ordinance to the teaching office of the Church."—*Canonical Provisions for Catholic Schools,* pp. 151, 152.

[84] Ordinariis locorum ius et officium est vigilandi ne in quibusvis scholis sui territorii quidquam contra fidem vel bonos mores tradatur aut fiat."

[85] "Eisdem similiter ius est approbandi religionis magistros et libros; itemque, religionis morumque causa, exigendi et tum magistri tum libri removeantur." Can. 1381, § 3.

[86] "Ordinarii locorum sive ipsi per se sive per alios possunt quoque scholas quaslibet, oratoria, recreatoria, patronatus, etc., in iis quae religiosam et moralem institutionem spectant, visitare; a qua visitatione quorumlibet religiosorum scholae exemptae non sunt, nisi agatur de scholis internis pro professis religionis exemptae."—Can. 1382.

[87] Cf. cans. 344, § 1; 1491, § 1.

[88] It is called a canonical visitation because it requires ecclesiastical jurisdiction and is prescribed by the Canon Law of the Church.—Pejška, *Ius Canonicum Religiosorum* (3. ed., Friburgi Brisgoviae, Herder & Co., 1927), p. 240.

common one among authors is given by Slafkosky [89] as follows: "Visitation is the act of making an inquiry into existing excesses and defects, punishing what needs chastisement, and amending with suitable remedies what is in need of correction, preserving the observance of prevalent obligations according to the requirements of every person and place, and restoring matters to their former condition wherever a relaxation has occurred." This administrative function provides the ordinary with a method of determining personally the nature and the manner of the religious instruction being given to youth in universities and colleges, and a control of the entire curriculum.[90] It gives him the opportunity also for immediate correction of the dangers or evils arising through textbooks or from teachers, even though they do not *ex professo* treat of religion. This is the right and the obligation of the local ordinary in all universities and colleges in his territory. This would be the ideal way of fulfilling the requirements of the law in a paternal fashion. In most dioceses, the number of universities and colleges would not be so great as to require the use of deputies by the ordinary. This ideal, however, is not realized at the present time.[91]

With the exclusion of a canonical visitation by the local ordinary or his deputy, and the denial of the canonical supervision

---

[89] *The Canonical Episcopal Visitation of the Diocese,* The Catholic University of America Canon Law Studies, n. 142 (Washington, D. C.: The Catholic University of America Press, 1951), p. 1.

[90] The primary concern at this point is with the powers of the local ordinary in respect to universities and colleges of a neutral or mixed character. It will suffice to make mention of the fact that the universities and colleges under the direction of regulars may be entirely exempt from the canonical visitation of the local ordinary by reason of privileges extended to the regulars by the Holy See. Cf. Leo XIII, const., *Romanos Pontifices,* 8 maii, 1881—*Fontes,* n. 582; Vermeersch, *Periodica,* XV (1926-1927), 57-61.

[91] This right of canonical visitation is not recognized even in Christian countries. Thus, the Concordat entered into by the Holy See with Italy in 1929 permits only an indirect supervision by the local ordinary in religious matters in the public schools on the elementary and intermediate levels. No provision for colleges and universities in this matter is agreed upon or even mentioned. Cf. Art. 36—*AAS, XXI* (1929), 291.

outlined above, the more extensive right and obligation of ordinary vigilance is not, thereby, wholly prevented.[92] There are many prudent and discreet ways of ascertaining the contents of the textbooks in use, and the material propounded in the lectures of the teachers. This right and obligation of "fact-finding" concerning the religious training of youth in universities and colleges of a neutral or mixed character remains incumbent on the local ordinary despite the practical impossibility of a strict canonical visitation and of a full exercise of the right of supervision in matters directly concerned with the religious instruction of youth.

The right of vigilance which as spoken of in the Code would place within the exclusive power of the local ordinary the selection of textbooks and the appointment of the teachers of religion, and their right to demand their removal if he should consider it necessary,[93] is not the ideal. Such supervision excludes any direct and immediate intervention on the part of the local ordinary. This right is also denied to local ordinaries by those who have charge of universities and colleges which are not immediately dependent on ecclesiastical authority. The writer knows of few private or State-controlled institutions for higher education which grant such supervision to the local ordinary of the territory.[94]

---

[92] Cf. Reilly, *The Visitation of Religious*, The Catholic University of America Canon Law Studies, n. 112 (Washington, D. C.: The Catholic University of America, 1938), pp. 124, 125, note 41; Boffa, *Canonical Provisions for Catholic Schools*, p. 180, note 82, and Slafkosky, *The Canonical Episcopal Visitation of the Diocese*, p. 82, note 36, who propose that visitation is the broader term, since the Code expressly mentions the situations in which visitation is to be included under vigilance (e.g. can. 1515, § 2). No difficulty arises, however, The writer is treating of the rights and obligations of the local ordinary, while these authors seek a precise distinction between the canonical terms. The right and obligation of ordinary vigilance over the universities and colleges in his territory does not cease for the reason that the ordinary is denied the right of canonical visitation.

[93] Can. 1381, §§ 2, 3.

[94] In summary, the following table will proceed from those countries in which a Concordat leaves the local ordinary excluded in the matter of a canonical visitation or of canonical vigilance in universities and colleges

to those countries in which there is an approach to the ideal expressed in the Code. Only those Concordats which have been entered into since 1918 will receive mention here.

Latvia, Art. 10—*AAS,* XIV (1922), 578. There is no mention of universities and colleges.

Poland, Art. 13—*AAS,* XVII (1925), 272, 278. Universities are excluded from the agreement to provide compulsory religious instruction for youth.

Italy, Art. 35, 36—*AAS,* XXI (1929), 291. No provisions were made for religious instruction in universities and colleges.

Roumania, Art. 19, 20—*AAS,* XXI (1929), 449. The supervision of textbooks and religious instruction is a matter for discussion and agreement between Ordinaries and the Minister of Public Instruction.

Germany, Art. 22—*AAS,* XXV (1933), 402. The ordinaries shall not have the right of visitation, but they may discuss provisions for the religious instruction of youth with the civil authorities.

Baden, Art. 11—*AAS,* XXV (1933), 187. The religious instruction which is given in schools is to be in conformity with Catholic doctrine and moral principles.

Bavaria, Art. 8, § 2—*AAS,* XVII (1925), 46. The religious instruction given in the schools is to be under the supervision of the ecclesiastical authorities, and any infractions are to be reported to the civil authorities.

Lithuania, Art. 13, n. 4—*AAS,* XIX (1927), 428. The provisions of canon 1381 are recognized in all public and state schools, i.e., the ordinaries may exercise their right of vigilance, but not their right of visitation.

Austria, Art. 6, § 2—*AAS,* XXVI (1934), 255. The ordinaries are given the right to supervise religious instruction and religious practices in the schools.

Portugal, Art. 21—*AAS,* XXXII (1940), 213. The textbooks used for the teaching of religion and the teachers of religion are subject to the approval of the ecclesiastical authorities. Without that approval, no one may teach religion in the schools. No express mention is made of universities and colleges. Cf. Bouscaren, *Digest,* II, 16, 17.

Spain, Art. 26, 27, 28—*AAS,* XLV (1953), 643-646.

Art. 26: All teaching in State or private universities and colleges is to be in conformity with the dogmas and principles of the Catholic Church. The Ordinaries are to exercise vigilance in the matter, and they may ask that materials opposed to faith and morals be removed. The civil authorities will carry out these requests.

Art. 27:

n.1. The Catholic religion is to be taught in the State colleges and Universities. Non-Catholic students may be excused from such courses at the request of their parents.

n.5. The teaching of religion in the universities is to be done by an ecclesiastic with a doctorate from a Catholic university, or its equivalent from a religious Order. His appointment shall come only after an examination by the local ordinary.

n.6. The professors of religion are to take full part in all the faculty meetings of the universities in which they teach. They may be removed by the ordinary for the reasons given in canon 1381, § 3. The civil authorities must hear the ordinary before they effect the removal of a teacher of religion.

n.7. All the teachers of religion in private schools must have a certificate of approval from the local ordinary. If the certificate is revoked, the right to teach religion is lost.

n.8. The schedule for the religious instruction of the students is to be fixed by the ecclesiastical authorities, and all the textbooks are subject to the approval of the ecclesiastical authorities.

Art. 28; n.1. Scholastic Philosophy, Theology and Canon Law may be taught in the State universities as long as the textbooks are approved by the ecclesiastical authorities. Priests, religious and laymen may teach the courses in these studies provided that they have secured a *"Nihil Obstat"* from the local ordinary.

The Dominican Republic, Art. 21, 22—*AAS*, XLVI (1954), 446-448.

Art. 21, n.1. The ecclesiastical authority is free to establish universities and colleges, and the civil government will accord them every protection. If need be, the civil government will aid in this work with financial grants. There is no permission required from the civil government to begin such schools. All the religious instruction is to be under ecclesiastical supervision.

n.2. The diplomas granted by the Ecclesiastical schools will be equal to those granted by the State schools.

Art. 22, n.1. The State schools must follow Catholic doctrine and Catholic principles.

n.2. The vigilance of the State is restricted to the requirements necessary for public health and the construction of buildings. The civil authorities must consult with the local ordinary before they undertake any corrections or changes.

n.3 When the number of priests is not sufficient to fill the need for teachers in the Normal Schools, the local ordinary is to decide which laymen are to be permitted to teach in those schools.

n.5. The right of visitation by the local ordinary or by his deputy is recognized.

There is no such right of supervision accorded to any local ordinary in the United States. In 1939, Pope Pius XII wrote to the Bishops of the United States concerning the American problem of education: "We raise Our voice in strong, albeit paternal, complaint that in so many schools of your land Christ often is depised or ignored, the explanation of the universe and mankind is forced within the narrow limits of materialism or of rationalism, and new educational systems are sought after which cannot but produce a sorrowful harvest in the intellectual and moral life of the nation."[95] In a radio address to the Inter-American Congress of Catholic Education in Bolivia in 1948, he urged the delegates to see to it that the children and youth, as they advanced in age, received a more ample and deeply rooted religious instruction. In their deliberations they were not to forget that both the full and profound consciousness of religious truth, as well as doubts and difficulties, usually manifested themselves in the last years of higher studies, especially if the student had come in contact with, as can hardly be avoided today, persons or teachings that are contrary to Christianity.[96]

Section 4. Delegation.

The prerogatives of the local ordinary as delineated in canons 1374, 1381, §§ 2, 3, and 1382 are part of his ordinary power, for he possesses them in his own right, by virtue of an office which he legitimately occupies.[97] As a part of his ordinary powers of

[95] Pius XII, litt. encycl., *Sertum laetitiae,* 1 nov. 1939—*AAS,* XXXI (1939), 650.

[96] Pius XII, nuntius radiophonicus, 10 oct. 1948—*AAS,* XL (1948), 466.

[97] Can. 197, § 1. Kearney, *Principles of Delegation,* The Catholic University of America Canon Law Studies, n. 55 (Washington, D. C.: The Catholic University of America, 1929), p. 76.

jurisdiction, the Code places it within the right of the local ordinary to commit these powers to another, who can then use them as the one designated in the name of the ordinary. Moreover, he may consign these powers to another in any measure and to any extent that he chooses,[98] since the Code does not add any restrictive clause to any of the canons in question. In fact, canon 1382 expressly mentions that the local ordinary may entrust the canonical visitation to others, *"sive per se sive per alios."* The conclusion that the local ordinary may commit his power with regard to the toleration mentioned in canon 1374, or his right of the vigilance warranted in canon 1381, §§ 2, 3, or also his right of canonical visitation as stated in canon 1382, or even all three of these in their entirety, proves a perfectly acceptable conclusion.[99]

Thus, the local ordinary could entrust the entire content of his rights in these matters to one of his priests, perhaps to the Superintendent of Schools. In most dioceses, however, the shortage of priests lamented by Pope Pius XII,[100] and the pressure of other duties would make it difficult for a single deputy to encompass such a large field of responsibility. If he were given a general unlimited concession of these powers, however, such a priest

---

98 "Qui iurisdictionis potestatem habet ordinariam, potest eam alteri ex toto vel ex parte delegare, nisi aliud expresse iure caveatur."—Can. 199 § 1.

99 Authors are generally agreed that a commission of the fulness of his power by an ordinary with no restriction of time or reservation of any power to himself would be equivalent to his resignation from office and the appointment of another in his place. This procedure on the part of the ordinary would require the consent of the pope as the only superior competent to permit such an action. Cf. Reiffenstuel, *Ius Ecclesiasticum Universum,* Lib. I, tit. XXIX, n. 56; Wernz-Vidal, *Ius Canonicum,* II, n. 369; Coronata, *Institutiones,* I, n. 288; Vermeersch-Creusen, *Epitome,* I, n. 318; Jone, *Commentarium in Codicem Iuris Canonici* (3 vols., I (1950), II (1954), III (1955), Paderborn: Ferdinand Schöningh), I, 199 (hereafter cited *Commentarium*). It is to be clearly understood that even a complete grant of his powers in the matters of the three canons above is by no means an abdication of the plenitude of his jurisdiction on the part of the local ordinary.

100 Pius XII, allocut., 14 oct. 1951—*AAS,* XLIII (1951), 786.

would be empowered by the Code to enlist, authoritatively, others to help him in his work.[101]

In practice, the right of a canonical visitation or the right of canonical vigilance on the part of the local ordinary is recognized in few places, as has already been seen. The vigilance possible to a local ordinary, in the United States at least, is only such vigilance as is possible to his pastors, who are restricted, for the most part, to gathering facts from others rather than acquiring them from personal observation in universities and colleges of a neutral or mixed character. For that vigilance, no pastor requires delegation from the local ordinary, since it is his obligation from the law in the Code.[102] In the matter of the toleration mentioned in canon 1374, it seems to the writer that the supreme legislator indicates a preference—it is not to be construed as an obligation on the part of any local ordinary—for a personal judgment from the local ordinary when he states: *"Solius autem Ordinarii loci est decernere."* This power may, in keeping with the rules of delegation as stated in canon 199, be delegated, even indeed in its entirety, by the ordinary to one of his priests, or to several priests, for the universities and colleges within the territory of the diocese.

Article 3. The Instructions of the Holy See.

At this point in the canonical commentary, one may well preface the treatment of the Instructions of the Holy See with an explanation of some pertinent facts. The research will show that in their greater portion, these Instructions were issued in the centuries already past. The Code, though it does not exclude the possibility of new Instructions, refers to documents which are not of recent origin.[103] The encyclical of Pope Pius XI on Christian

[101] "Potestas delegata ad universitatem negotiorum ab eo qui infra Romanam Pontificem habet ordinariam potestatem, potest in singulis casibus subdelegari."—Can. 199, § 3.

[102] "Parochus diligenter advigilet ne quid contra fidem ac mores in sua paroecia, praesertim in scholis publicis et privatis, tradatur . . ."—Can. 469.

[103] Cf. the footnote to canon 1374, in which the documents cited are from the years 1659 to 1910. In the field of modern education, that which

Education, which has been called "the veritable Charter of Christion Education by Pope Pius XII,[104] was not intended to be a new definition of the Catholic position. Pope Pius XI sought, in his own words, "to summarize its [Christian Education] main principles, to throw full light on its important conclusions, and to point out its practical applications."[105] Those principles are not new. They are part of the heritage of Christianity. It was the need for an application of those principles to concrete circumstances in given areas of the Church's universal jurisdiction which gave rise to the several Instructions of the Holy See. Some will say that the Church has not kept pace; that the Instructions of the Holy See, so timely in the past, have outlived their usefulness; that times, circumstances, needs and methods have changed radically, so that the law refers to norms which were issued for other times and other places. A consideration of the most recent papal pronouncements coupled with some of the declarations of those who seek to restore religious education to the universities and colleges of a neutral or mixed character will serve to discredit such a theory about the Instructions of the Holy See.

From the current declarations of those who are entrusted with the religious and the spiritual interests at private, non-sectarian universities and colleges in America, two facts are clear. They note that on college and university campuses all over America there is a great "revival of interest" in religion. The nature and the character of the particular religion is yet vague, but the commentators are agreed that it is a complete reversal of the attitude of the 1930's on the same campuses. Inasmuch as the current statements reflect a recent revival, it must be expected that the statements are terse and brief rather than the equivalent of a published treatise. They are, however, for that reason, not less valuable for the present purpose. They indicate the position and the trend of religious thought in these universities and colleges.

The report of the Carnegie Corporation of New York, a re-

---

borders on the half-century mark seems to be thought of as truly characterizing an old vintage.

[104] *L'Osservatore Romano,* September 5-6, 1955.

[105] Encycl., *Divini illius Magistri—AAS,* XXII (1930), 50.

search organization,[106]—"gave a preview of a survey made by four Cornell sociologists of 7,000 students at twelve colleges and universities. Of those questioned, eight out of ten said that they feel a need for a religious faith. Only 1% described themselves as atheists. Though the tendency, said the report, is not toward any particular creed, today's students seem fairly well agreed that there must be some religious system based on God as the Supreme Being." This points up the revival of interest among the majority of students in universities and colleges, and just as clearly the confused notion of what constitutes the basic elements of a "religious system," as it is termed in the report. The number of students enrolled in the courses of religion at these private universities and colleges is increasing.[107] The new and enthusiastic[108]

---

[106] The summary of this report is from *Time,* the Weekly News Magazine (New York, Time, Inc.), vol. LXVI, No. 21 (Nov. 21, 1955), p. 60.

[107] Yale in 1933 had 3 courses in religion with only 4 students in Biblical Literature. In 1955, there are 12 courses and 400 students in Biblical Literature. Princeton, in 1939, in its first religion course had 20 students. Now, 700 students are enrolled in various courses. The number of Smith [College] girls enrolled in religion courses has doubled to 442 since 1950.—*Time, ibidem,* pp. 61, 62. It is reported of Princeton that "the even tenor . . . has been rudely jarred by a religious controversy. . . . Central to the present phase of the struggle are Princeton's Department of Religion and the Rev. Hugh Halton, O.P., chaplain to Catholic students. Fr. Halton has challenged the professional competence of the nine members of the department—none of whom is a Catholic or has made a formal study of Catholic philosophy or theology—to lecture on the Catholic religion. Since this department enjoys the status of a liberal-arts department, and since, as Fr. Halton points out, 'Catholicism is specifically (though not exclusively) taught in more than 45 percent of the courses,' his point seems valid. Several members of the department are ordained Protestant ministers. All members preach by turn in the University chapel. A required text in the department is Joseph Fletcher's *Morals and Medicine.* The Dominican chaplain, in a full-page ad in the Feb. 9th issue of the *Daily Princetonian,* riddled the scholarly pretensions and vicious errors of this book."—*America,* National Catholic Weekly Review (New York, The America Press), Vol. XCIV, No. 22 (Feb. 25, 1956).

[108] Though the new enthusiasm is not yet universal, almost every campus has felt it 'I've been in the dean's office for more than 20 years,' says Nicholas McKnight, dean of students at Columbia College, "and never have I seen such a wide interest in religion among the students.'—*Time, loc. cit.*

student-interest in religion is ascribed to a variety of reasons including fear, doubt and a search for a solution to modern-day problems.[109]

---

[109] "Revolt or not, says the Rev. George Buttrick, Harvard's professor of Christian morals, 'the cycle has come full turn. Once we doubted our faith. Now we have come to doubt our doubts." The overwhelming reason for this is 'the threat of nothingness' brought on by the atomic bomb. Adds William D. Geohegan, assistant professor of religion at Bowdoin College: 'The resurgence of religion is largely due to the shock administered to cultural Couéism by two world wars, a depression, and the painful knowledge that the great powers possess the awesome tools of genocide. Religion is seen as an essential tool in the hard work of sheer survival, not as a matter of icing on the cake.'

For the most part, one of the dominant characteristics of the new young Christians is not their concern with social service but their preoccupation with finding themselves. 'Religiously,' says Clarence P. Shedd, emeritus professor of Christian methods at Yale, 'it is a wistful generation, tired of living on snap judgments and seeking enduring foundations. . . . This does not mean a return to religion or a revival of religion. Rather it means that these students are seeking to come to grips with the basic problems of faith and living. They are asking not superficial but ultimate questions, and they will not be satisfied with easy answers. They want to find solid grounds for ultimate loyalties.'

In their search for solid grounds, the students have not surrendered their right to criitzice, nor do they seem any more susceptible than their parents to blind acceptance of dogma. As a matter of fact, says Kaare Roald Bergethon, dean of the college at Brown University, the students seem so tolerant of the beliefs of others that 'if I had seen this same phenomenon in the 30's, I would have thought it was indifference, but today I know it isn't.' This tolerance has meant that old gods have not been dethroned; they have merely been demoted. 'Science students,' says Goucher's Director of Religious Activities, Walter Morris, 'have come to realize that science is accurate and true in those areas to which it has purposely limited itself.' Freud is still studied respectfully, but he no longer monopolizes the conversation. The fashion now, says Nicholas Cardell, director of the University of Chicago's Unitarian Channing Club, 'is to talk of Niebuhr or Tillich.'

Once again religion has become intellectually respectable. 'In my day,' says David Webster, acting dean of men at Temple University, 'we were apt to say that religion is a superstition.' Today, says Chaplain Richard Unsworth of Smith College, 'theology is no longer classed with domestic science as a subject not suited for a liberal arts college.' . . . On campus after campus, says Amherst's James Martin, 'there is what one might call

The position of college and university presidents in the matter of religious education, of education for competence, and of the training of conscience will, doubtless, run the gamut of possibilities between and including those expressed by Nathan M. Pusey of Harvard[110] and John Sloan Dickey of Dartmouth.[111] In the universities which are state-controlled, and hence are public schools, it may be expected that religious education will follow the policy repeated in the White House Conference on Education (Dec. 7, 8, 9, 1955), unless there has been special provision made in some states.[112]

In modern-day America, then, there is a growing demand for

---

at least a new look at the values of our Hebrew-Christian heritage, not only as a neglected and important factor in our cultural history, but also as a possible source of faith for living in today's world—or yesterday's, or tomorrow's.' "—*Time, ibidem,* 61, 62.

[110] "It is ironical and sad that religion—a subject of central concern when Harvard College was founded—should have steadily, if imperecptibly, lost ground in the modern period to a point where, despite several courageous rear-guard actions, it was threatened with extinction. Today it is almost universally acknowledged that the study of religion rightfully belongs [within universities], and that this is so because religion's concerns make valid claims upon us all."—*America,* No. 22 (Feb. 25, 1956), p. 575.

[111] In 1951 Dartmouth started a special foundation named after its ninth president, William Jewett Tucker. Its purpose: to foster the spiritual life of the campus and to help students meet President Tucker's challenge: 'Seek, I pray you, moral distinction.' Thus, says Dickey, is Dartmouth grappling with liberal education's major twin concerns. 'I have no interest,' says he, 'in seeing the liberal-arts become too precious for the man who hungers after competence. But it is the job of the college to keep competence civilized . . . I rate very highly the fact that in the liberal-arts college neither competence nor conscience is taken straight. Rather, it is the human interplay between these two poles of purpose that gives liberal education its orientation to the lights and brings to the undergraduate grown a man those liberating and civilizing qualities men never quite define nor even quite deny.' "—*Time, Vol.* LXVI, No. 23 (Dec. 5, 1955), p. 51.

[112] "At 10 on Tuesday morning the round-table discussions began. By that evening, the final report on Topic 1 was ready. What should the schools teach? Just about everything it turned out. . . . As might have been expected, the Conference sidestepped the question of whether religion should be taught in the public schools."—*Time,*Vol. LXVI, No. 24 (Dec. 12, 1955), p. 68.

formal religious education on the college and the university level. What it seeks to accomplish is a matter of conjecture. It seems that, in most instances, non-Catholic students are at the moment seeking a religion without a creed or dogmas. Should the "revival" continue along such lines, then Arnold Toynbee's conception of Christianity and Revelation[113] will, perhaps, come into prominence and be acceptable and accepted in light of the American desire for "tolerance."

Does this revival serve to show that the dangers from a secular concept and practice of education which flourished in the early decades of this century are things of the past? Are the threats from Communistic teachers and from professors who openly ridiculed "the myth of God" no longer in evidence? Such seems to be not yet true. In 1954, the Bishops of America in their annual statement pointed up the fact that the sought-after faith had been reduced to emotion or sentiment from the necessary conviction that it must be "knowledge in its highest form," with God Himself as the guarantor of its truths. This "revolt" on the part of the students must prove itself to be more stable and permanent than it seems to be at present, in order that it overcome the objections of a non-Catholic observer made in 1949.[114]

Pope Pius XII has spoken often and written much about the matter of education on the college and university level. He seeks,

---

[113] "Christianity must purge itself of accidental Western accessories. We treat Christianity as if its virtue were not derived from being Christian, but from being Western. . . . One can believe that one has received a revelation without necessarily believing he has received exclusive revelation. Exclusive-mindedness is one of the most fatal sins . . . the sin of pride. . . . I suggest that we recognize all higher religions as revelations of what is good and right."—*Time,* Vol. LXVI, No. 20 (Nov. 14, 1955), p. 83.

[114] Bernard Iddings Bell considered that the popular "Religious Emphasis Week" conducted by many universities and colleges gave him "a right to be indignant when a university which encourages its students to sell their potentialities in sacrificial love for a mess of pottage has the effrontery to bid them remember briefly, four days a year, the primacy of God. There are limits to a properly tolerated indecency. . . . It makes an honest man angry to see a university indifferent to ethics."—*The Crisis in Education* (New York, Whittlesey House, 1949), p. 157.

as did his predecessors, a return to the primary principles and objectives of a truly Christian education, "in accordance with the wisdom and experience of the Church in matters of teaching and, especially, with the norms promulgated by this Apostolic See."[115] This message radioed to the Inter-American Congress on Education held in La Paz, Bolivia, in 1948, is a model of clarity and a careful repetition of the Church's position at the present time.

> May Our most fervent prayers reach unto the throne of the Most High that from this Congress there may come forth, definitively organized, a Confederation whose purpose is to see to it that the education of youth in all the American countries is carried on, conscientiously and efficaciously, in accordance with the wisdom and experience of the Church in matters of teaching and especially with the norms promulgated by this Apostolic See. In this way it may rise to that dignity and that splendor that must impel the authorities and citizens of your respective peoples to recognize the liberty and to grant the respect to which the teaching institutions of the Catholic Church have the right.
>
> But this Congress of yours has still another attraction: the theme which you have so wisely chosen for your deliberations: "Education and the Modern Environment."
>
> The essence and the goal of education—to use the expression of Our immediate Predecessor—consist in collaboration with divine grace for the formation of the true and perfect Christian. In this perfection is included the ideal that the Christian, as such, be in condition to face and to overcome the difficulties and to correspond to the demands of the times in which it is his lot to live. That means that the work of education, since it must be carried on in a specific environment and for a specific background (*milieu*), must constantly adapt itself to the circumstances of this background, and of this environment wherein this perfection has to be obtained and for which it is destined.
>
> See that you children and your youths, as they advance

[115] Pius XII, nuntius radiphonicus, 10 oct. 1948—*AAS,* XL (1948), 466.

> in age, receive religious instruction that is accordingly more ample and more deeply-established; not forgetting that both the full and profound consciousness of religious truths, as well as the doubts and difficulties, usually manifest themselves in the last years of higher studies, especially if the student has to come into contact, as can hardly be avoided today, with persons or teachings that are contrary to Christianity. For this reason, religious instruction demands with every right a place of honor in the programs of universities and centers of advanced studies.
>
> See to it that with this instruction there go, closely united, the holy fear of God, the habit of undistracted prayer, and the full and intelligent participation in the spirit of the Liturgical Year of Holy Mother Church, the source of countless graces. But in this work, act with caution and prudence, so that it will be the youth himself who will always be seeking something more and, little by little, working by himself, will be learning to live and to practice his life of faith.[116]

He has serious proposals for Catholic educators and university students in other parts of the world also. In 1949, in an audience with hundreds of professors and students from several universities in France,[117] he reminded them that among the great concerns of the Holy See was the great disorder It sees in the minds of moderns. He makes it part of their duty before God and before men to preserve and to pass on the treasures of knowledge and intelligence with which they have been endowed by the Father of Wisdom. In the world's preoccupation with the fascination for knowledge, the desire to know all things, and the contentment with the superficial benefits of a disparate knowledge, there is danger. Without the preparation and the preliminaries which are necessary for an orderly and fruitful appreciation and application of that which they desire to know, students are engaged in the

[116] *Loc. cit.* Translation by the NCWC News Service, Editorial Information.

[117] i.e., The Sorbonne, Paris, Lille, Angers, Toulouse, Lyons, Bordeaux, Nancy and Grenoble.

intellectual fields of philosophy, sociology, economics and the physical sciences. From it all will come not truth, but a disposition to sophism and error. The remedy for these evils is to come from them as the intellectuals and the writers of France. The Holy Father bids them to remember that a writer or an intellectual must consider himself as *"homo missus a Deo . . . ut testimonium perhibeat de lumine."* (John I, 7, 8). The dignity with which God has clothed him must move the writer and the intellectual to a great respect, a respect above all for the Eternal Light from Whom he has received a mandate to project His reflection on all creation, and a respect for truth, in order that he may never alter, mutilate or discredit truth because of passion, fear or vain ostentation. From an educattion which provides them with these ideals and abilities, they can and they must have a great part in solving the problems of others not so fortunate by giving them a sound, healthy, intellectual nourishment.[118]

Fundamental to any system of Christian education must be the recognition of the existence of human conscience and the need for training the human conscience in the laws of Christian morality. These principles are the object of another significant radio address, made by Pope Pius XII in 1952.[119] His descriptive definition of conscience places it into an important position for consideration by all those who give serious thought to the vital components of a truly Christian education. "Conscience may be described as the innermost and hidden center of man's being. There he takes refuge with his spiritual faculties in absolute solitude; alone with himself or better still, alone with God—Whose voice conscience echoes—and with himself. There he decides for good or evil; there he chooses to set foot either on the road to victory or on the road

[118] "Il n'y a qu'un remède: repondre au besoin et à l'appel des intelligences, en leur donnant, en leur accomodant, une nourriture saine, substantielle, qui les dégoûte des breuvages capiteux et de mets frelatés. La èst la difficulté, maís la èst la beauté, la grandeur de votre rôle."—*Discorsi e Radiomessagi di Sua Santità Pio XII,* 1939—, XI (2 Marzo 1949—1 Marzo 1950, Romae: Tipografia Poliglotta Vaticana), pp. 39-41.

[119] Pius XII, nuntius radiophonicus, 23 mart. 1952—*AAS,* XLIV (1952), 270-278.

to defeat. Even if he wished, man would never succeed in getting rid of conscience. In the company of his conscience, whether it approve or condemn, he will travel all the way along the path of life and, again, in its company, as with a truthful and incorruptible witness, he will present himself before the judgment-seat of God."[120]

There can be no clear understanding of how conscience can and ought to be educated, according to the Holy Father, without a going back to certain fundamental concepts of Christian doctrine. Jesus Christ's execution of the Divine Plan of Redemption brought many things to men. Among them were truth and grace. Man, if he was to reach his supernatural end, needed truth to show him the way to his goal and grace to help him to reach it. In making his way to his supernatural goal, a man must, in practice, accept the will and the commandments of Christ in such a way that he conforms his life to the precepts left by Christ. Conscience is the spiritual faculty which points out to the will, for its choice and decision, the actions which are in conformity with the Divine Will. The ultimate and deciding norm for a moral action must be taken from the teaching and the Will of Christ.

From these truths follows the highest duty of education, namely, the forming of the Christian conscience of youth. That formation must consist, before all else, in enlightening the minds of youth regarding the Will of Christ, His law and His way. Thus will the youth be enabled to act upon their inner self in order to bring that inner self to the free and constant compliance with the Divine Will.

The Holy Father then proceeds to outline the prerequisites and sources for the education of the conscience. He reminds educators and those to be educated that the Christian moral law can be found concretely and with ease and certainty. It exists in the natural law engraved on the hearts of men by the Creator, and in Revelation, the whole body of truths and precepts taught by Christ. As a moral treasure for mankind, these sources of the moral law have been entrusted to the Church, in order that it may preach them to all creatures, make them clearly known and hand them over intact and uncontaminated by error from one

120 *Loc. cit.*

generation to another. These are, in outline, the doctrines from which the Church has drawn the necessary and basic elements of a Christian education.

A "new morality," as the pope terms it, has arisen to challenge the position of the Church. They want a moral law which is free from the sophistic subtleties of the casuistic method. They want the moral law in its original form, and left simply to the intelligence and determination of each man's individual conscience. This is hardly the natural climate for a Christian conscience. Truth, the very basis for any conscience which can hope to be Christian, was entrusted not to individuals but to the Church. Grace, as a divine aid meant to preserve Revelation free from error, was promised to the Church, and not to individuals. To remove conscience from these necessary safeguards and to surrender it to a kind of individual autonomy can bring forth only poisonous fruits in private as well as in public life.

The Pope concludes with an exhortation to those who are engaged in the work of educating youth:

> "Educate the consciences of the young in fear as well as in the love of God, and in truthfulness. Impress upon the consciences of the young the genuine concept of freedom which is truly worthy of a creature made to the image of God. This is a proved disposition for good; it is that self-decision to will what is good and to accomplish it; it is the mastery of one's own faculties, of instincts, of events. Educate them to prayers and to the Sacraments to draw that which nature cannot give: the strength not to fall, the strength to rise again. Let them know from youth, that without the aid of the supernatural energies of the Sacraments they cannot succeed in being either good Christians or even honorable men, whose heritage is a serene life. Thus prepared, they will be able to aspire to what is best, to give themselves to the great personal task, whose fulfillment will be their boast, to make Christ live in their lives."[121]

---

[121] *Ibidem*, pp. 277, 278. The translation is from *Catholic Documents* (London: The Salesian Press, 1950—), VIII (1952), 5.

The function of a university was clearly outlined by Pius XII as one that cannot change even though it should find it necessary to add new subjects to its curriculum and to enlarge its facilities. In a letter to the 22nd World Congress of *Pax Romana* in Montreal,[122] he declared his purpose to be that of defining the directives he had given for intellectuals in remembrance of the decisive action of the Roman Pontiffs in the origin of the first universities and in their subsequent courses through the centuries. The present-day world seeks to sever the age-old links between the universities and the Church. For the spiritual good of the world, those links must be re-established and the universities themselves can help to bring it about if they will work prayerfully for the true mission of universities.

(1) A university must be a community of teachers and students which is dedicated to works of the spirit, radiating intellectual life for the benefit of the nation in an atmosphere of healthy freedom.

(2) A university is to render fruitful for the new generations the centuries-old treasures which it has received in deposit.

(3) A university is to bring together men and peoples in a peaceful intellectual collaboration achieved in the unity of truth.

(4) A university is not merely a place at which there is an attempt at the juxtaposition of abilities which are foreign to one another, but a place wherein men strive for a synthesis of all the objects of knowledge.

(5) Modern specialization renders this synthesis more difficult and more fragile and the university must protect it from two dangers:

a. The undue interference of the State which would presume to impose on education, for political or ideological ends, the specious unity of an arbitrary philosophy;

b. The confinement to a plane of mere natural knowledge with its difference of subjects, and the consequent failure to promote wisdom and a respect for truth.

Only Catholic universities, illumined in their task by Faith, can pursue the efforts for synthesis, for this unity will tend toward

---

[122] Pius XII, litt., 12 aug. 1952—*AAS*, XLIV (1952), 728, 730.

its perfection only in the measure in which it seeks itself in God, in charity illumined by knowledge, according to the single truth of the Gospel, under the guidance of the Church which is one and holy. Such universities, crowned by the teaching of Christian philosophy and theology, and at the service of the young student, will be schools of truth; they will also be mistresses of life, Christian, moral, civic and social.[123]

The present position of religious instruction in the American universities and colleges of a neutral or mixed character has two possible completions. Either the revival of "religous interest" will be temporary and these universities and colleges will once more adopt a neutral or, in some cases, a hostile position to any organized course of religious instruction, or the revival will grow and take definite shape and pursue its quest for a religion without dogmas and culminate once more in Indifferentism, Naturalism or Secularism, as such movements have in the past. Both possibilities present serious dangers to the faith and morals of the Catholic students who desire to attend such universities and colleges.

These dangers are not new, nor are they, uniquely, American. The Holy See was concerned with the same dangers many years ago. These dangers were the concern of the Holy See before the Councils of Baltimore saw fit to point them out as existing in the field of higher education in America. It will be seen that the Instructions of the Holy See which are referred to in canon 1374 were dealing with the same double problem, an educational philosophy and environment which was in some cases openly hostile to the Church, and in other cases completely indifferent to the

[123] "Mission délicate, toute de fermeté et de discrétion, à laquelle Nous convions spécialment Nos Universités catholiques, illuminés dans leur tâche par les splendeurs de la foi, elles seules peuvent poursuivre l'effort de synthèsis jusqu'à la clé de voûte de l'edifice, car 'cette unité ne tendra vers sa perfection que dans le mesure où elle se cherchera en Dieu, dans la Charité éclairée par la science, selon la vérité unique de l'Evangile sous la conduite de l'Eglise une et sainte.' Au service de la jeunesse étudiante, de telles Universités, couronnées par l'enseignement de la philosophie chrétienne et de la théologie, seront des écoles de vérité; elles seront aussi des maîtresses de vie, chrétienne, morale, civique et sociale."—*AAS, ibidem,* p. 730.

Church's principles for the imparting of a truly Christian education. As norms for the application of the law of the Church to concrete situations, the Instructions are timeless and readily adaptable to the circumstances in which local ordinaries find Catholic students on the university and the college level.

The norms which the legislator requires the local ordinaries to consider in their deliberations before coming to a decision about the possibility of a decree of toleration for the attendance of Catholics at universities and colleges of a neutral or mixed character are the following:

(1) The bishops are to warn parents and students of the dangers arising from attendance at universities or colleges of a netural or mixed character through their own preaching and that of their priests, and through pastoral letters.[124]

(2) The bishops are to give urgent consideration to the erection of Catholic colleges despite any opposition which may come from heretics or schismatics, and to constitute them on a plane equal to those established by the civil government.[125]

(3) The possibility of sending the students to Catholic universities and colleges in other areas is to be carefully considered and weighed."[126]

(4) In the event of co-operation proffered by the civil government for the erection and the maintenance of Catholic universities and colleges, the bishops are to accept such financial grants only when the conditions imposed by the civil governments are not contrary to faith or morals.[127]

(5) The desires on the part of the parents or of the students for worldly prestige or merely temporal benefits are of no consideration in this matter.[128]

(6) The attendance of Catholics at universities or colleges of a

---

[124] S.C. de Prop. Fide, litt. encycl., 6 aug. 1867—*Fontes*, n. 4868; Leo XIII, ep. encycl., *Quod multum*, 22 aug. 1886—*Fontes*, n. 594.

[125] S.C. de Prop. Fide, litt. encycl., 21 mart. 1865—*Fontes*, n. 4863; S.C. de Prop. Fide, instr., 8 sept. 1869—*Fontes*, n. 4876.

[126] S.C.S. Off., instr., 21 mart. 1866—*Fontes*, n. 992.

[127] S.C. de Prop. Fide, instr., 25 apr. 1868—*Fontes*, n. 4873.

[128] S.C. de Prop. Fide, litt. encycl., 6 aug. 1867—*Fontes*, n. 4868.

neutral or mixed character may be tolerated by the ordinary when a consideration of the foregoing norms fails to provide a solution, and as long as the following conditions are true:

a. The bishop, the priests and the parents will join in a concerted and concentrated effort to remove the dangers to the faith and the morals of the Catholic students.[129] by providing for their religious instruction at least after school hours.[130]

b. The bishop shall try to secure his right to seek the removal of textbooks or teachers who are manifestly opposed to Catholic principles and to Catholic doctrines.[131]

c. The bishop shall appoint inspectors to aid him in his obligation of vigilance over the books, the teachers and the curricula of the universities and the colleges in his territory.[132]

(7) In those universities and colleges which are erected and controlled by the civil government, the bishop must strive to see to it that all education is in complete harmony with the Catholic faith in its literature and system of teaching, particularly in the field of philosophy.[133]

(8) The bishop must exercise great care and vigilance in the matter of the religious instruction which is given in the Normal schools which provide the future teachers in his territory,[134] and he must insist that the Catholic students in those schools be taught religion, history and moral subjects by Catholic teachers only.[135]

(9) In those classes which are common to all of the students at the university or the college, only profane subjects shall be taught with no admixture of truths which are labeled as fundamental to all religions.[136]

10. "When the right education of youth is concerned, no

---

[129] S.C.S. Off., instr., 21 mart. 1866—*Fontes,* n. 992.

[130] S. Pius X, Litt. encycl. *Acerbo nimis,* 15 apr. 1905—*Fontes,* n. 666.

[131] Leo XIII, Ep. encycl. *Caritatis providentiaeque,* 19 mart. 1894—*Fontes,* n. 623.

[132] Leo XIII, Ep. encycl. *Constanti Hungarorum,* 23 sept. 1893—*Fontes,* n. 620.

[133] Leo XIII, Ep. encycl. *Inscrutabili,* 21 apr. 1878—*Fontes,* n. 573.

[134] Leo XIII, allocut. *Summi Pontificatus,* 20 aug. 1880—*Fontes,* n. 581.

[135] S.C. de Prop. Fide, litt., 16 ian. 1841—*Fontes,* n. 4787.

[136] *Loc. cit.*

amount of trouble or labor can be undertaken, no matter how great, but that even greater still may not be called for."[137]

The III Plenary Council of Baltimore (1884) exhorted parents to send their children to Catholic colleges. The Fathers of the Council decreed that toleration for the attendance of Catholics at colleges of a neutral or mixed character—the Pastoral Letter of the same year shows that the colleges other than the Catholic ones had become secular in their philosophy and in their teaching[138]—could be extended only in the event that a certain course of study was not offered by the Catholic colleges, and only after the parents had been warned of the serious obligation they assumed for making as remote as possible the dangers to the faith and morals of their child.[139]

It is important, as a point of law, to establish the nature and the force of the Instructions of the Holy See, for they show that the prohibition of canon 1374 is not absolute, and that the toleration which may be conceded by the local ordinaries is conditioned, and consequent upon the norms outlined above. The norms established in these Instructions from the Holy See proceed not only from papal documents, but also from the communications of the Sacred Congregations.[140] The binding force of the Instructions dispatched by the Sacred Congregations to particular countries or areas before 1917 is a point for discussion among authors. Briefly, the history of the origin of the legislative power as an additional grant to the Sacred Congregation of the Council begins with the action of Pope Pius V in 1564,[141] and then proceeds through

---

[137] "Cum de fingenda probe adolescentia agitur, nulla opera potest, nec labor suscipi tantus, quin etiam sint suscepienda maiora."—Leo XIII, Litt. encycl. *Sapientiae christianae,* 10 ian. 1890—*Fontes,* n. 605.

[138] Guilday, *Pastorals,* p. 230.

[139] *Acta et Decreta,* N. 210.

[140] "Nomine Sedis Apostolicae vel Sanctae Sedis in hoc Codice veniunt non solum Romanus Pontifex, sed etiam, nisi ex rei natura vel sermonis contextu aliud appareat, Congregationes, Tribunalia, Officia, per quae idem Romanus Pontifex negotia Eccelsiae universae expedire solet."—Can. 7.

[141] This summary of that history is drawn from the article by J. R. Schmidt, "The Juridic Value of the *Instructio,*" *The Jurist,* I, (1941), 289-316.

several declarations by succeeding Popes until, in 1908, St. Pius X made it clear[142] that all the Sacred Congregations were to continue in their capacity as administrators and executors of the law, and that they were to be authentic interpreters of the law, each within its own competence. The function of authentic interpretation of the canons of the Code was reserved to the Pontifical Commission for the Authentic Interpretation of the Code by Benedict XV in 1917.[143] For the present purposes it suffices that the force of the Instructions of the Sacred Congregations was always considered to be at least juridic, namely, an exercise and an expression of the executive and the administrative function accorded to these agencies by the supreme legislator.[144] As executive measures, the norms and the directions of the Instructions are ordinances whereby laws are translated into action in specific cases or situations; they are obligatory in conscience, and they can be enforced by means of penalties.[145]

It is in the light of these Instructions that the local ordinary is to consider the particular circumstances in his territory, and the safeguards which prove feasible for the removal of the danger of perversion to the Catholic students.

Section 1. Circumstances.

The circumstances may be grouped under four headings for the sake of convenience: the courses of study which the student desires; the student's geographical situation; the financial condi-

---

[142] S. Pius X, const. *Sapienti Consilio,* 29 iun. 1908—*Fontes,* n. 682.

[143] Benedictus XV, *motu proprio, Cum iuris canonici,* 15 sept. 1917—*AAS,* IX (1917), 483, 484. It is the third document inserted at the beginning of the reprints of the Code of Canon Law.

[144] "Instructiones quoque SS.CC. nequaquam per se et indiscriminatim vim legum universalium et definitionum habent. Nam 19 Sept. 1761: '*De mandato Sanctissimi* (Clementis X) *iniunctum fuit, quod quotiescumque missionariis ceterisque S. C. de Prop. Fide ministris mittuntur resolutiones dubiorum factae a S.C.S. Off. et Propag. Fidei, non mittantur tamquam DEFINITIONES, sed tamquam simplices INSTRUCTIONES,* quibus in occurentibus dubiis gubernari valeant et debeant.' Cfr. Collectan. (Paris.) Const. S. Sed. n. 5."—Wernz, *Ius Decretalium,* I, n. 146.

[145] Cf. Schmidt, "art. cit.," *The Jurist,* I (1941), 314, 315.

tion of the student and of his parents, and the available facilities for the actual acceptance of the Catholic student in a Catholic university or college. It will be remembered that the III Plenary Council of Baltimore[146] had decreed that toleration for the attendance at universities or colleges of a neutral or mixed character by Catholic students was to be conceded only in the event that the existing Catholic colleges did not offer a certain desired course of study. The number of courses of study which are not actually offered in Catholic universities and colleges has certainly been appreciably decreased since the year of 1884 in which the Council was held. When one considers the geographical situation of the student in relation to the nearest Catholic university or college, a distinction must be made. When the student in question is one who will be a boarding student, the expenditure and the inconvenience of travel need not be a great factor in the ordinary's decision in the light of what will, ordinarily, be a negligible difference because of the rates and the modern means for travel. Should the attendance of the student at a Catholic university or college, in relation to his attendance at a university or a college of a neutral or mixed character, involve a reasonable amount of sacrifice on the part of his parents and himself, that sacrifice is to be made. In like manner, the student who seeks to commute to his daily classes at a university or a college of a neutral or mixed character is to be given consideration by the ordinary in relation to the Extensions or Divisions of a Catholic university or college which may exist nearby. A strong consideration in the ordinary's deliberations will be the difficulty which arises from the concrete situation in which the parents and the student find that they cannot afford the attendance of the student at a Catholic university or college at which, by reason of distance, it is imperative that the student be a boarding student, while they can manage to supply the means necessary for the student's attendance at the nearby university or college of a neutral or mixed character. With regard to financial matters in general, when reasonable sacrifice will compensate for the difference in the expenses to be incurred by attendance at a Catholic university

146 *Acta et Decreta,* N. 210.

or college as compared with the expenses to be incurred by attendance at a university or college of a neutral or mixed character, then the financial conditions are not to be a serious consideration in the ordinary's decision. The number of vacancies in the Catholic universities or colleges at the beginning of a given scholastic year will be an important point in the determinations of the ordinary. The apparently difficult problem created when a Catholic high school graduate is awarded a scholaship to a university or college of a neutral or mixed character will find adequate solution in the Instructions and in the considerations delineated above, joined with what follows in the discussion of the safeguards to be employed against the danger of perversion.

Section 2. Safeguards.

The safeguards requisite for making remote the occasions for moral evils and for lapses from the faith on the part of Catholic students in universities and colleges of a neutral or mixed character may be placed under three classes of activity: the practice of the Catholic faith on the part of the Catholic students; their participation in courses of religious instruction, and the measures which may be taken by the local ordinary. The ordinary will be in a position to provide facilities which will be nearby for the use of the students for prayer and for frequent reception of the Sacraments of Penance and the Most Holy Eucharist, along with the careful supervision of zealous priests. In the matter of religious instruction, it may well be the case that Credit-Courses or Non-Credit Courses in Religion, supplemented by lectures and discussion groups, are offered in the university or college which the student desires to attend.[147] In those places in which such a

[147] Such Credit-Courses are given at the Universities of Iowa, Illinois, North Daktoa, and at New York University and Bradley University. Credit-Courses are also given at Michigan State College and Youngstown College. Louisiana State University, The University of California, the University of Pennsylvania, Cornell University, Vanderbilt University, Wayne University, Western Reserve University, Peabody College, Case Institute of Technology any Dyke College offer Non-Credit Courses to Catholic students. Cf. *The Newman Club in American Education* (Washington, D. C., The National Association of Newman Club Chaplains, 1953), pp. 11-21; 22-29.

system is not yet in existence, the ordinary or his delegate could well explore the possibilities of making such provisions, since the frequent association between students and priests would provide the ordinary with a close check on the religious and moral conditions in the universities and colleges in his territory.

There are universities and colleges of a neutral or mixed character which attempt to exclude any supervision by or co-operation with the ecclesiastical authority. Other universities and colleges may have textbooks or faculty members who are either hostile to or contemptuous of the Catholic Church. In that event, it is submitted by the writer as a suggestion that in the case of a State university the authorities might well be apprised of the fact that Constitutional guarantees are being violated through the use of certain textbooks and the lectures of certain teachers. In respect to private universities or colleges which follow a similar course in which there is danger to the faith and morals of its Catholic students, a reminder from the ordinary or his delegate that such a practice is offensive to the minority group of Catholics and to their parents because of its attacks on things of the spirit might prove very useful. Although such action on the part of the ordinary is not likely to remove all the dangers, it may well serve as a brake against continuous or unrestrained attacks on the Church in the presence of Catholic students.

Article 4. The Decree of the Local Ordinary.

After learning the conditions in each university and college of a neutral or mixed character in his territory, and after giving them careful consideration in their relation to the Instructions of the Holy See, the local ordinary may determine to grant toleration for attendance at such universities and colleges in his diocese only after a discussion or appraisal of each individual case. He may insist that such a plan be executed by himself, personally, or by his delegate. It may be his decision to give a determination for all cases by the promulgation of a decree to his pastors empowering them to make the decision in individual instances in accordance with the sufficient reasons and the necessary safeguards as determined and communicated to his delegates by the ordinary himself.

The promulgation of a decree of toleration by the local ordinary which would insist that every case of a Catholic seeking toleration for attendance at a university or college of a neutral or mixed character be referred to himself, personally, would bring the canonical effect of reserving to himself exclusive competence in this matter. In that event, no pastor, confessor, theologian or inferior of the local ordinary could grant the toleration necessary for such an enrollment or attendance. It would also be beyond their powers to give an efficacious judgment on the merits of any case without an express delegation from the local ordinary. Should it be the latter's decision to constitute some of his priests as his delegates, they would be obliged to withhold all concessions of toleration in the cases which did not fulfill the conditions established by the ordinary. In those cases in which they did extend toleration, they would be required to make periodic investigations in order to ascertain any changes in the conditions set by the local ordinary, which changes would deprive their decrees of their force.

The promulgation of a decree by the local ordinary certainly seems to be the intention of the legislator from the words of canon 1374: *"decernere . . . tolerari possit."* These words, taken in the sense of requiring a decree of toleration, exclude tacit toleration on the part of the ordinary. This opinion is given a strong probability because of the words *"decernere . . . tolerari possit,"* and because of the fact that in issuing a decree of toleration the local ordinary is obliged to promulgate the conditions under which the toleration is to be conceded. As such, then, there can be no tacit toleration, i.e., a toleration which did not acquaint his subjects with the determined conditions.[148]

Even after the local ordinary has determined that a given university or college of a neutral or mixed character is not directly opposed to Catholic tenets of Christian doctrine or Christian morality, but rather makes a conscientious effort to remain neutral—

[148] Cf. Blat, *Commentarium,* Liber III, pars IV, n. 257.

a practical impossibility as a constant procedure—he is faced with the difficult problem occasioned by the fact that he is concerned with individuals of different backgrounds, environments and character. What will prove to be of no proximate danger to the faith or to the morals of one Catholic of university or college age may well be disastrous for another. Thus, to encompass within the application of a single rule or norm, a large number of relatively immature young people who have been reared in a society which does not understand the meaning of education in the terms of a truly Catholic education is a task requiring great wisdom and discretion. The writer speaks here of the Catholic youth in America. They and their parents, as parish priests and college and university chaplains can well attest, in most cases are convinced that a college education is meant to provide the means for social and economic advancement only. Attendance at the "right" college or university will bring a measure of the prestige which they deem necessary for the "good" life in America. They have not been educated to the idea of a university or a college education as a means for advancing in the spiritual life through a diligent, prayerful application to study and to recreation.[149] Contrast this with the statements of Pius XII and the great disparity is evident.

> Counteract the lack of principles of the world today, which measures everything by the criterion of success, with an education which makes a youth capable of discerning between truth and error, good and evil, right and injustice, planting firmly in his soul the pure sentiments of love, fraternity and fidelity.
>
> To the exaggerated importance that is accorded today to whatever is purely technical and material reply with an education which always gives first place to spiritual and moral values; both to the natural and, above all, to the supernatural ones. The Church, without any doubt whatever, approves of physical culture, if it be in proper proportion. It will be in

---

[149] Cf. Maguire, "Another Look at Subversion of Faith," *America*, Vol. XCII, No. 10 (Dec. 4, 1954), p. 271.

such proportion when it does not lead to a worship of the body, when it is useful to strengthen the body and not to dissipate its energies, when it serves also as a recreation for the spirit and is not a cause of spiritual weakness and crudeness, when it supplies new incitements for study and for professional work and does not conduce to their abandonment or neglect or to disturbance of the peace that should reign in the sanctuary of the home.

Immoderate pursuit of pleasure and lack of moral discipline likewise seek to invade even the ranks of Catholic youth, trying to make them forget that they bear within themselves a fallen nature weighed down with the sad legacy of original sin. Counteract this with the education of self-control, of sacrifices and of renunciation, beginning with smaller things and gradually going on to greater ones; education of fidelity in the fulfillment of one's own duties, of sincerity, serenity and purity, especially in the years of development into maturity. But never forget that it is impossible to reach this goal without the powerful help of the Sacraments of Confession and of the Most Holy Eucharist, whose supernatural educative value can never be duly appreciated.

Develop in the souls of children and youths the hierarchical spirit—which does not deny to each age its proper development—so as to dissipate, as far as possible, this atmosphere of independence and excessive liberty which our youth breathes in today and which would lead it to throw off all authority and every check. Try to arouse and to mould a sense of responsibility and to remind them that liberty is not the only one among all the human values, although it is numbered among the foremost, but that it has its limits, intrinsic in the unescapable norms of decency and extrinsic in the correlative rights of others, both as regards the rights of each one in particular as well as the rights of society in general.

Not rarely the parents themselves need special help, since oftentimes they have not themselves received the necessary preparation for the exercise of their educative duties; and upon a good understanding with them will ordinarily depend

> the success of education, however good the schools may be, and even though the teachers be the best.[150]

Culpably or not, students and parents are not aware of the dangers from attendance at a university or a college which is other than Catholic. The local ordinaries of America cannot give that awareness to their subjects in any way save through a long and consistent process of re-education, while they seek the means to enlarge the present facilities for education on the university and college level. In the meantime, they are faced with no general problem, unless it be considered that, in the circumstances and conditions peculiar to each diocese, the constant and general element in the attendance of Catholics at universities and colleges of a neutral or mixed character is the one of danger to their faith and to their morals. The danger will however be particular, as to degree, in each case.

It has been said that the words *"decernere . . . tolerari possit"* leave no room for tacit toleration. It is not meant, however, that every ordinary must issue a decree of toleration as the Code may seem to call for. In fulfilling his obligation of ordinary vigilance, the facts which come to light may serve to make it plain to the local ordinary that he is faced with the moral impossibility of making a prudent and an effective application of the positive law of canon 1374 because of the serious evils which would result. In his deliberations, it may become evident that a decree of toleration for subjects who are unaware or unconcerned at present about the dangers to the faith or to the morals of Catholic students from their attendance at universities or colleges of a neutral or mixed character would evoke only disobedience or even disregard of his law in this matter, and this spirit of non-compliance could readily broaden in relation also to some of his other laws. A prudent, even though uneasy, silence with careful attention to all of the measures which would help to remove or to make remote the dangers may prove a wise, though temporary solution. In such circumstances, namely, when no decree of toleration has been is-

[150] Pius XII, nuntius radiophonicus, 10 oct. 1948—*AAS,* XL (1948), 468, 469 (Translation by NCWC News Service, Editorial Information).

sued by the local ordinary, pastors and other priests may offer a prudent judgment in individual cases. It is always an opinion only that is given, and it does not impose any strictly canonical obligation on the students or their parents. Nor is it to be considered as a decree of toleration which retains its force in the event of a future decree from the local ordinary.

It remains now to consider the legislation of the III Plenary Council of Baltimore in this matter in relation to the law of the Code. From the wording of canon 1374, and from the previous discussion it is clear that only the local ordinary or his delegate may determine the matter of toleration for the attendance of Catholics at universities or colleges of a neutral or mixed character.[151] The III Plenary Council of Baltimore, in 1884, left that judgment to the parents of the student when it was found that a desired course of study was not offered by the Catholic colleges which existed at that time.[152]

This *particular* law of the III Plenary Council of Baltimore, then, permitted that which now is prohibited by the *universal* law of the Code. Since there is no clause in canon 1374 which would retain the prior particular law, the prescription of canon 6, 1°,[153] requires that the law of the III Plenary Council of Baltimore be considered as abrogated.

---

[151] "Solius autem Ordinarii loci est decernere, ad normam instructionum Sedis Apostolicae, in quibus rerum adiunctis et quibus adhibitis cautelis, ut periculum perversionis vitetur, tolerari possit ut eae scholae celebrentur."—Can. 1374.

[152] *Acta et Decreta,* N. 210—" . . . parentes in Domino hortamur, ut adolescentes suos, quibus, scholis parochialibus absolutis, superiorem educationem procurare velint, in Catholicas scholas superiores jam nunc existentes mittant. Si vero scholae Catholicae filiis suis pro speciali quem sequuntur studiorum cursu desint eosque ob hanc causam in scholas acatholicas mittere cogantur, enixe eos monemus, ut fidei morumque pericula a filiis suis quam longissime removeant, verbi Domimi semper memores: 'Quid prodest homini si mundum universum lucretur, animae vero suae detrimentum patiatur.' (Matth., XVI, 26)."

[153] "Leges quaelibet, sive universales sive particulares, praescriptis huius Codicis oppositae, abrogantur, nisi de particularibus legibus aliud expresse caveatur."

CHAPTER VI

The Attendance of Non-Catholics at Catholic Universities and Colleges.

At first glance it may appear that an interpreter of law is overreaching himself in treating the question of this chapter. In the careful, universal systematization of Canon Law as it is found in the Code of Canon Law, the legislator offers no express treatment of the question of the attendance of non-Catholics at Catholic universities and colleges. There is no canon in the Code which regulates their admittance as to number. There is no canon which provides for a distinction as to the position of the legislator in relation to non-Catholics who are not baptized, and those who are, when there is question of their attendance at Catholic universities and colleges. There is no canon which makes explicit provision for the manner and the nature of the religion instruction which non-Catholics are to receive as students in a Catholic university or college. There are, however, laws in the Code and also pre-Code Instructions from the Sacred Congregations which provide an interpreter with norms for the solution to the questions which arise in view of the actual practice among non-Catholics of attending Catholic universities and colleges.

Prior to a discussion of the problems proposed above, it seems to the writer that it will be of service to the reader to have before him a repetition of some pertinent and basic concepts of law and of Christian doctrine for a better understanding of the solutions which will be given. For non-Catholics, such a brief exposition may, perhaps, help them to see the reasoning behind the position taken by the writer.

Law in general, in any of the three accepted definitions which are proposed here,[1] has for its basic purpose the strict government

[1] St. Thomas Aquinas defined law as a "regulation in accordance with reason promulgated by the head of the community for the sake of the

and the forceful direction of the members of a society to a determined end. The expression of the lawful superior's mind and intention for the purpose of securing that end will be found in the law which he communicates to the members of the society. His law will be something stable, reasonable, possible of observance, and for the common good of the members of the society, rather than for the private good of any individual.

For Catholics, the great divisions of society are determined by the twofold end of man as a creature of God. Man's first entrance into society is into that portion which is called the family. Because of the social nature of man, families have bound themselves into another unit of society which is called the State. Both the family and the State will help him, if he wills to be helped, to a measure of temporal happiness, which is one of the ends of his existence. Since man is also pointed to another end, a supernatural one, he is in need of supernatural aids because of his damaged nature which is the result of sin or moral evil. He is, then, under the government and the direction of three lawful superiors; the head of the family, the head of the State, and God.

In the plan of Redemption, the God-Man, Jesus Christ, was to provide the society which would have the lawful authority to govern, direct and aid men to the attainment of their supernatural end, namely, the possession of eternal happiness. That society is called the Church. That Church, like its Founder, possesses all the means necessary to accomplish its purpose. The function of the Church is a social one, one which is to benefit the whole of Society. Man, in his life on earth, needs supernatural truth to give his life purpose and direction to his supernatural end, and he requires grace or supernatural aid from God if he is to reach his supernatural end. For the former, the Church is endowed by Christ with jurisdiction, and for the latter with the power of orders.[2] The function of the Church in respect to supernatural

---

common welfare." According to Suarez, law is "a general precept, just and stable, promulgated in a sufficient manner." Law is defined by D'Annibale as "a permanent, general command properly promulgated by a lawful superior for the welfare of his subjects." Cf. Cicognani, *Canon Law,* p. 521.

[2] Cappello, *Summa Iuris Publici Ecclesiastici,* p. 183.

truth is designated with the term *magisterium,* which singles out the doctrinal prerogative of the Church whereby it controls the belief of its members as well as their behavior. Part of that *magisterium* of the Church will be, obviously, to acquaint men with the teaching of its Founder, Jesus Christ.

It is that right to exercise the function of teaching which must be vindicated for the Church. That mission is a divine one imposed upon the Church in the form of legislation by its Divine Founder.[3] It is divine law, the result of a divine mandate given by the Supreme Legislator to the Apostolic College and to their successors, which obliges the Church to its divine mission of teaching the truths revealed by Christ. It is responsible for the *propagation* of the Deposit of Faith, for the *preservation* of that Deposit, and for the *defense* of that Deposit.

Men must be taught that in their own efforts, in working for the attainment of their supernatural end, they must follow the truths and the principles contained in the Deposit of Faith, and that they must be governed also. Just as Christ was both a Teacher and Lawgiver exercising His divine prerogative, so, too, He endowed His Church with the same power of teaching and of making law in order that the Church be able to exercise the function of government over men in matters pertaining to their eternal salvation.[4] The Code of Canon Law states the position of the

---

[3] "And Jesus drew near and spoke to them [the eleven disciples], saying, 'All power in heaven and on earth has been given to me. Go, therefore, and make disciples of all nations, baptizing them in the name of the Father, and of the Son, and of the Holy Spirit, teaching them to observe all that I have commanded you; and behold, I am with you all days, even unto the consummation of the world." Matth. 28: 18-20. "At length he appeared to the Eleven as they were at table; and he upbraided them for their lack of faith and hardness of heart, in that they had not believed those who had seen him after he had risen. And he said to them, 'Go into the whole world and preach the gospel to every creature." Mark, 16: 14-16. *The New Testament of Our Lord and Savior Jesus Christ* (The Episcopal Committee of the Confraternity of Christian Doctrine, Paterson, N. J.: St. Anthony's Guild Press, 1941), pp. 90, 145.

[4] "And I say to thee, thou art Peter, and upon this rock I will build my Church, and the gates of hell shall not prevail against it. And I will give thee the keys of the kingdom of heaven; and whatever thou shalt

Church in relation to the divine mandate of Christ by insisting that the Deposit of Faith was confided to it exclusively, and for the purpose of preserving and expounding the revealed doctrines in the Deposit.[5] The Church maintains further that, independently of any civil powers, it has the right and the obligation to teach all nations the doctrines of its Founder from His positive divine law, and that all men are bound, in virtue of that divine mandate, to acquire a proper knowledge of Christ's doctrine and to embrace the true Church of God.[6] For the security of the men who seek to do the Will of God, His Church teaches under a guarantee, granted by Christ, which makes it free from error in matters of faith and morals.[7]

The position of the Roman Pontiff as the one possessing the plenitude of jurisdiction in the exercise of the teaching function of the Church, and the position of the local ordinary as the one rendering the immediate judgment in the matter of Catholic education have been discussed in the preceding chapter.[8] In his diocese or territory, the local ordinary is the one who has the right and the obligation "to rule the Church of God as a successor of the Apostles."[9] In the exercise of the teaching function of the

---

bind on earth shall be bound in heaven, and whatever thou shalt loose on earth shall be loosed in heaven." Matth., 16: 18-20—*Ibidem,* pp. 48, 49. Cf. Wernz-Vidal, *Ius Canonicum,* I, n. 122.

[5] "Christus Dominus fidei depositum Ecclesiae concredidit, ut ipsa, Spiritu Sancto iugiter assistente, doctrinam revelatam sancte custodiret et fideliter exponeret."—Can. 1322, § 1.

[6] "Ecclesiae, independenter a qualibet civili potestate, ius est et officium gentes omnes evangelicam doctrinam docendi; hanc vero rite ediscere veramque Dei Ecclesiam amplecti omnes divina lege tenentur."—Can. 1322, § 2.

[7] "Fide divina et catholica ea omnia credenda sunt quae verbo Dei scripto vel tradito continentur et ab Ecclesia sive sollemni iudicio sive ordinario et universali magisterio tanquam divinitus revelata credenda proponuntur."—Can. 1323, § 1. Cf. Wernz-Vidal, *Ius Canonicum,* I, n. 123.

[8] Cf. Article 2.

[9] Acts, 20: 28; Conc. Trident., sessio XXIII, *de ordine,* c. 4—Schroeder, pp. 161, 162; "Episcopi sunt Apostolorum successores atque ex divina institutione peculiaribus ecclesiis praeficiuntur quas cum potestate ordinaria regunt sub auctoritate Romani Pontificis."—Can. 329, § 1.

Church, the local ordinary, under the authority of the Roman Pontiff, is the official teacher in his diocese or territory.[10] He is constituted in this role by divine law, and all others who engage in the work of the teaching authority and the teaching function of the Church within his territory serve in the capacity of aides to the local ordinary.[11]

The means at the disposal of the Church for the exercise of its teaching function include the propagation of revealed truths through schools and formal education.[12] A part of that teaching function in a given territory will be assumed by the Catholic colleges and universities established there. In that event, the judgment concerning the instruction and the education to be imparted by the Catholic colleges and universities in his territory is within the ecclesiastical jurisdiction of the local ordinary alone. Unless they are properly delegated, it is not within the province of those

---

[10] "Episcopi quoque, licet singuli vel etiam in Conciliis particularibus congregati infallibilitate docendi non polleant, fidelium tamen suit curis comissorum, sub auctoritate Romani Pontificis, veri doctores seu magistri sunt."—Can. 1326.

[11] Leo XIII, ep., *Officio Sanctissimo,* 22 dec. 1887, n. 6: "Hoc munus permagnum *quod est exhortari in doctrina sana, et eos qui contradicunt arguere* (Tit. I, 9), ad ordinem pertinet sacerdotum, qui legitime habuerunt a Christo Domino impositum, quum divina ille potestate dimisit ad gentes universas docendas: *Euntes in mundum universum, praedicate evangelium omni creaturae* (Marc. XVI, 15); ita plane ut episcopi, in Apostolorum locum sublecti, praesint magistri in Ecclesia Dei, presbyteri adiutores accedant."—*Fontes,* n. 596.

[12] The other means are:

1. Infallible definitions which are solemn definitions of revealed truths, and the proscription of errors by the Roman Pontiff alone or by the Roman Pontiff and an Ecumenical Council.—Canon 1323, § 2.

2. Preaching of the word of God by those who are commissioned to do so by legitimate authority in the Church.—Can. 1328.

3. Books and other writings, which are either positive promotions of truth, or positive condemnations of error, in keeping with the Church's divine mission.—Can. 1384.

4. Professions of Faith on the part of those who are obliged to do so by reason of their position, or because of the circumstances which may arise.—Canons 1352, § 1; 1406.

who aid the local ordinary as teachers or administrators in Catholic universities or colleges to make these determinations.[13]

The presence of non-Catholic students in a Catholic university or college calls for an exercise of the teaching authority and the teaching function of the Church in all three of its branches, as it were. Non-Catholic students in the classrooms of Catholic universities and colleges present an opportunity for the *propagation* of revealed truth. The same mixture of Catholic and non-Catholic students in one school also places the Catholic students in danger with regard to their faith and morals, and it may also require the Church to take steps for the *preservation* and the *defense* of the revealed truths contained in the Deposit of Faith. It is true that the dangers which arise from the employment of teachers and textbooks which are not Catholic are not present in most Catholic universities and colleges. The possible weakening of the faith and the morals of the Catholic students from their unavoidable associations with the non-Catholic students, however, cannot be denied or ignored. It is the fact of a different and a particular approach on the part of non-Catholics to matters of faith and morals which has given the Church cause for concern. Non-Catholics obviously do not believe as Catholics, and this difference in matters of faith and morals is not without its influence on the Catholic students in attendance at the same school.

The determination of the policy to be adopted and followed by the Catholic universities and colleges concerning the non-Catholics who seek to attend these schools is to come from the local ordinary or his delegate. In canon 1374, the Code requires that, in matters of education on the higher level, his primary concern

---

[13] "Religiosa iuventutis institutio in scholis quibuslibet auctoritati et inspectioni Ecclesiae subiicitur."—Can. 1381, § 1.

"Ordinariis locorum ius et officium est vigilandi ne in quibusvis scholis sui territorii quidquam contra fidem vel bonos mores tradatur aut fiat."—Can. 1381, § 2. The canonical constitution of a Catholic university as a Pontifical University empowered to grant ecclesiastical degrees is reserved to the Holy See.—Can. 1376, § 1. There is one such university in the United States of America, the Catholic University of America in Washington, D.C., which was erected as a Pontifical University by Pope Leo XIII on March 21, 1889.—Cf. *Acta Sanctae Sedis,* XXI (1889), 517.

must be to protect his Catholic subjects from the dangers to their faith and morals, the *periculum perversionis,* even though the circumstances in his territory force from him a reluctant and an unapproved toleration of their attendance at colleges or universities of a neutral or mixed character. It is the exposure of Catholic students to the influences from teachers, books and fellow students who are not Catholic which imposes this obligation on the local ordinary. The obligation derives from the divine law, and the Code of Canon Law only reaffirms the right and the obligation and makes it the concern of the local ordinary alone, unless he delegates his powers. In the present consideration, the dangers to the faith and to the morals of Catholic students from their exposure to the influences emanating from non-Catholic students are not removed simply because the associations among the students are now made within the confines of a Catholic university or college. They are reduced, but not obviated. The fact of the danger remains, although the degree of the danger is reduced. It is no violation of the principles of law, then, to maintain that a similar careful concern is required on the part of the local ordinary in his deliberations with respect to the number and the character of the non-Catholic students who are to be permitted to attend the Catholic universities and colleges in his territory. Once admitted to a Catholic university or college, the nature and the content of the religious instruction to be given to the non-Catholic students must be determined by the local ordinary. The matters to be discussed now lend themselves quite readily to a division into two Articles: the proportionate number of non-Catholics who may be admitted to Catholic universities and colleges, and the religious instruction to be imparted to those who are admitted.

Article 1. The Proportionate Number of Non-Catholics Who May Be Permitted to Attend Catholic Universities and Colleges.

This is a matter which offers a measure of difficulty to the local ordinary. Conscious of his obligation as deriving from the divine law, he is also confronted with the consideration that the Catholic universities and colleges in his territory are the results, for the most part, of the generosity of the Catholic faithful. On both counts he must be solicitous for the spiritual welfare and for the faith and the morals of the Catholic students in those universities and colleges. Anything less than a judicious determination concerning the proportionate number and the character of the non-Catholic students who are to be admitted to the Catholic universiies and colleges can give rise to numerous possibilities for associations which will prove dangerous for the Catholic students. It has been said that most Catholic university and college students are not aware that there are dangers from such a condition. That fact only serves to heighten the need for care in the matter. The local ordinary cannot be unmindful of the fact that the non-Catholics in his territory are bound by the divine law as it is stated in canon 1322, § 2, even though some of them are not validly baptized. They are bound to observe the divine law as it is declared by the Church, and to refrain from placing any obstacle which would impede the Church from securing its objective in the matter of bringing the Gospel to all men through the use of its teaching authority. They are bound also to observe the divine law which grants to the Church the right and the obligation to protect its baptized members from dangers to their faith and morals.[14]

The Holy See has issued Instructions in the past when the conditions and the circumstances in a particular territory prompted the ordinary to place his problems before one of the adminstrative agencies of the Holy See.[15] From these applications of the law in

[14] "*Leges divinae positivae* pariter omnes tenent; leges vero, quae natura sua baptismum supponunt, ut sunt leges quae respiciunt receptionem aliorum sacramentorum quaeque eam ob rationem solos baptizatos directe obstringunt, non-baptizatos indirecte ligant, suscepto scilicet baptismo, ad quod directe obligantur.—Notetur in specie quod *non-baptizati ex ipso iure divino* tenentur ad servandum ius divinum, naturale et positivum, *prout ab Ecclesia declaratur* et ad non impedienda jura a Christo Domino Ecclesiae, ut finem suum obtineat, concessa, puta quoad praedicationem Evangelii (cf. can. 1322, § 2) vel quoad propriorum subditorum defensionem."—Michiels, *Normae Generales,* I, 346, footnote 1.

[15] Some authors maintain that these Instructions constitute laws in the strict sense. Thus, Boffa in *Canonical Provisions for Catholic Schools,* pp. 121, 122, and Guay in "Fréquentation des écoles non-catholiques," *Revue de l'Université d'Ottawa,* VII (1937), 49*. For this writer, since the

particular cases, the local ordinary is provided with the norms he is to use in making the determinations concerning the proportionate number of non-Catholic students who may be admitted to the Catholic universities in his territory.

The question of the proportionate number of non-Catholics who may be admitted to the Catholic schools was proposed to the Sacred Congregation of the Holy Office in 1866 by the ordinary of Lwow. It seems that, for some years before, the practice of admitting the daughters of schismatics into a boarding-school for girls had been a habit with the religious who directed the school. The schismatic girls never numbered more than one-third of the entire student-body at any time, and in the year in question they constituted one-third of the total number of students enrolled. They took all their classes with the Catholic girls, and they were instructed in the Catholic religion. They were free to attend the spiritual exercises along with the Catholic girls, but they were not obliged to do so. These facts were known to the parents of the schismatic students. The ordinary was concerned about the continuance of such a practice and he placed the problem before the Holy See.

The solution was given by the Sacred Congregation of the Holy Office in a number of precise directions. The number of schismatic girls who comprised one-third of the student body was to be tolerated as long as they were of good character. Those who desired to visit these girls were required to seek the permission of the ordinary unless they were the parents or the guardians. The ordinary was to be vigilant in order that no danger of loss of faith or of weakening of morals or of lapse into indifferentism arise for the Catholic students from their associations with the schismatic girls in attendance at the school.[16]

This answer in its application was confined to the conditions obtaining in a school for young girls, and it is reasonable to pre-

---

Instructions to be considered were, in each instance, issued by Sacred Congregations other than the Sacred Congregation of the Council, and likewise were issued before the *Sapienti Consilio* of St. Pius X in 1908, the incontrovertible fact about them is that they have juridic force, at least.

[16] S.C.S. Off., 11 iun. 1866—*Collectanea,* n. 1292.

sume that the Holy See did not picture a group on that age level (elementary grades) as presenting any organized or concentrated threat to the faith or to the morals of the Catholic students in a well-disciplined boarding-school under the direction and control of religious. The response, nevertheless, was most cautious and circumspect.

In a lengthy Instruction, which was intended to be a resumé of former Instructions on the matter of non-Catholics' attendance at Catholic schools, the Sacred Congregation for the Propagation of the Faith included the norms which local ordinaries were to follow in the same matter when there was question of students on the college level. The Sacred Congregation required[17] that the following information be submitted for its judgment when a local ordinary sought a response to a particular difficulty. The scope of the college was to be outlined along with the quality and the grade of instruction which was being given there. With a reminder that it had required a careful investigation into the character of the children of parents who were heretics in Moscow and in Egypt before such children were admitted to Catholic schools, the Sacred Congregation insisted that it be informed of the number of non-Catholics who sought admittance to Catholic colleges, and also of the proportion of the entire student-body represented by that number. In 1883, the same Sacred Congregation when issuing an Instruction to the Vicars Apostolic in China urged the erecting of a Catholic college for each of the five vicariates. Only Catholic students were to be admitted to these colleges. Any exceptions to this general rule would be made by the Sacred Congregation itself, and only after it had considered the full particulars in each case as it was reported to the Sacred Congregation by the Vicar Apostolic.[18]

There was no fixed, permissible proportion of non-Catholic students to be admitted to Catholic colleges established by the Holy See. The American Bishops at the III Plenary Council of Baltimore (1884) recognized the dangers from the attendance of

---

[17] S.C. de Prop. Fide, 25 mar. 1868—*Collectanea,* n. 1329.

[18] S.C. de Prop. Fide, instr. (ad Vic. Ap. Sin.), 18 oct. 1883—*Fontes,* n. 4903.

non-Catholic students in Catholic colleges. Their decree in this matter made it clear that, although such attendance was not absolutely prohibited, the greater the number of non-Catholics in a Catholic college, the more the necessity for vigilance was increased.[19] The constant reference to the danger for the Catholic students from a possible infection with the ideas of indifferentism, rationalism or naturalism arising from religious discussions or disputes among the Catholic and the non-Catholic students in a Catholic university or college serves to mirror the concern of the Church over the presence of a vocal and aggressive non-Catholic minority in these schools. In the opinion of the writer, this is the grave danger, especially in the Catholic colleges in America. The struggle against indifferentism as a spiritual evil which influences college and university students is always much more difficult than the one which the local ordinary must wage against the evil of heresy. It is the position of the writer that no fixed, mathematical proportion for the number of non-Catholic students who may be admitted to Catholic colleges and universities has been given by the Holy See, for the reason simply that all too often the local circumstances of an ordinary's territory would make such a determination dangerous to the faith and to the morals of the Catholic students. It is submitted, however, that a proportion of non-Catholic students in the measure of one-third of the entire student-body will, ordinarily, place the Catholic college or university in danger of losing its nature and its power of influence as a truly Catholic university or college.

The ideal of the Church in this matter has not changed. Pope Leo XIII repeated to the bishops of Austria, Germany and Switzerland that it is the chief aim of the Church to have Catholic schools with competent, approved teachers, and that admittance should not be permitted to non-Catholic students.[20] Pope Pius XI,

[19] "Quamvis alienos recipere non absolute prohibeamus, enixe tamen superiores hortamur ut moribus omnium alumnorum eo religiosius invigilant, quo magis permixti sunt, ut non solum Catholici ab acatholicis nullum detrimentum, sed nec acatholici a Catholicis ullum scandalum patiantur."—*Acta et Decreta,* N. 213.

[20] Leo XIII, ep. encycl., *Militantis Ecclesiae,* 1 aug. 1897—*Fontes,* n. 635. This statement of Pope Leo XIII has great significance when it is

when speaking of nations in which there are different religious beliefs, sought a system of public instruction which would leave Catholics free to follow their own system of teaching in schools which would be entirely Catholic.[21]

When the Church has permitted the attendance of non-Catholic students in Catholic universities and colleges, it has come about as the result of careful consideration of serious reasons, or because of obstacles placed in its way.[22] The local ordinaries in a nation

---

remembered that it was precisely in Austria, Germany and Switzerland that the ruinous tendencies which had been brought on by the laws enacted during the period in which the cultural revolt of the *Kulturkampf* confused the minds of so many civil authorities were still exerting a great measure of influence. This movement had its origins in the Deism of France, in the Josephinism in Austria and in the excessive devotion on the part of German Liberals to some rationalistic German poetry and philosophy. They spoke and wrote about a Christianity without dogmas and without ecclesiastical authority. They were opposed to all churches and to all positive belief. In the Grand Duchy of Baden, all ecclesiastical influence in the schools was removed in favor of "free science" in 1860. By 1870, under Bismarck, all the important government positions in Prussia and Germany were held by Liberals. The civil supervision over schools was extended to all religious instruction in 1871. Many of the teaching Orders were forced to leave in 1872, and the infamous "Falk Bill," in which the term *Kulturkampf* was first used, was passed in 1873. It was to place education, even that of the clergy, under the control of the State along Liberal lines. All religious instruction was to be given by teachers who were appointed or approved by the civil authorities. Even after Leo XIII and Bismarck had entered upon a program which would bring some peace between the Church and the State, Bismarck insisted on State-control for the schools. —Cf. Martin Spahn, *The Catholic Encyclopedia,* VIII, 703-710; H. J. Heuser, "Prince Bismarck's Conflict with the Catholic Church," *The American Catholic Quarterly Review* (48 vols., Philadelphia, Hardy and Mahoney, 1876-1923), IX (1884), 322-339.

[21] Pius XI, Ep. encycl. *Divini illius Magistri,* 31 dec. 1929—*AAS,* XXII (1930), 78.

[22] An illustration in point can be found in an Instruction sent to the Bishop of Jassy in Roumania in 1900. The Sacred Congregation of the Holy Office began its Instruction with the statement that circumstances in a particular place may make it inexpedient to forbid the attendance of non-Catholics at Catholic schools. The circumstances in Roumania at that time, as well as in all the countries under the rule of Francis Joseph I of Austria, were not favorable to a system of education which would give the

as diverse and complex in conditions and circumstances as is the United States of America are obliged to consider the dangers arising from the attendance of non-Catholics at Catholic universities and colleges in their own territories, and it is conceivable that their determinations as to a safe, proportionate number of non-Catholics who may be admitted to Catholic universities and colleges will vary. The faith and the intelligence of the Catholic students and their lack of an awareness of the dangers outlined above, coupled with a consideration of the religious or irreligious mentality of the non-Catholics in his territory, may well call for a policy of restriction and for an increase of vigilance as to the proportionate number of non-Catholics who may be admitted to the Catholic universities and colleges in his territory. The dangers have not grown less. The vigilance cannot decrease.

Article 2. The Religious Instruction of Non-Catholics Who Attend Catholic Universities and Colleges.

The divine law in this matter is clear. The Church, in the exercise of its divinely commissioned teaching authority and teaching function, is obliged to teach the revealed truths in the Deposit of faith to all men.[23] It has been seen that the Catholic universities and the Catholic colleges serve as a means for that exercise under the authority of the Roman Pontiff and the local ordinaries. In order that a Catholic university or college be a fit instrument

---

Church the direction of the schools of Roumania. The objectives of the *Kulturkampf* were effected in Austria by that country's Liberal Party. For that reason, the Sacred Congregation of the Holy Office was moved to reply to the Bishop in Jassy that the attendance of non-Catholics at Catholic schools was to be tolerated. (Cf. Tschuppik, *Francis Joseph I, The Downfall of an Empire* [trans. by C. J. S. Sprigge, New York: Harcourt, Brace and Co., 1930], pp. 183, 187). That toleration was permissible as long as the practice of admitting non-Catholic students to Catholic schools would not obliterate or nullify the Catholic character of those schools, and that the faith and the morals of the Catholic students were not impaired.—S.C.S. Off., instr., 22 aug. 1900—*Fontes,* n. 1245.

[23] Matth., 28: 19; Mark, 16: 16; Can. 1322, § 2.

for this work it is necessary that it have certain qualities and that it be able to perform certain functions. These necessary elements have been given a precise and a detailed description by Pope Pius XI.[24]

All of the teaching and the entire organization of the university or college, namely the appointing of its teachers, the arranging of its curricula and the choosing of the textbooks in every branch of learning must be regulated in accord with the true Christian spirit. All these things must be under the direction and the maternal supervision of the Church, in order that religion may be truly and actually the foundation and the crown of the youths' entire training. Before him, Pope Leo XIII had required that the religious instruction of youth was not to be confined to certain class hours only, but that Christian piety was to permeate all the other subjects which are taught. For Leo XIII, if a holy atmosphere did not pervade and warm the hearts of the teachers and the students alike, little good could come from any learning, and considerable harm would often be the consequence.[25]

That this divine mandate given to the Church is at times impossible of fulfillment in Catholic schools may be illustrated from the Instruction sent to the Bishop of Jassy in Roumania in 1900, which was mentioned in connection with the discussion in the preceding article. It has been seen that the civil government, dominated by the Liberals in Austria, had usurped the ecclesiastical authority even in the Catholic schools and had forced the bishops to admit non-Catholic students into the Catholic schools. The Catholic schools were also compelled to employ non-Catholic teachers. Even under these conditions the Sacred Congregation of the Holy Office instructed the bishop that the teaching of metaphysics, ethics and all moral subjects was to be done by Catholics only, and that all textbooks, particularly those which had been written by non-Catholics, were to be examined carefully for any likely errors in them. The religious instruction of the schismatic

---

[24] Ep. encycl., *Divini illius Magistri,* 31 dec. 1929—*AAS,* XXII (1930), 77.

[25] Leo XIII, ep. encycl., *Militantis Ecclesiae,* 1 aug. 1897—*Fontes,* n. 635.

students by schismatic catechists was to be given, if at all possible, in a place apart from the Catholic schools. The bishop was reminded that the Church expected that he and has fellow-bishops would continue their efforts to see that only Catholic doctrine was taught to Catholic and non-Catholic students alike in all Catholic schools.[26]

The civil laws of the United States place no restriction on the Church in regard to the religious instruction imparted in Catholic colleges and universities. The lack of clarity in the matter of Church and State and Religious Education revolves about public education, and not private education.[27] The Federal government and the governments of the respective States have not interfered in the matter of religious education in private and in Catholic universities and colleges since 1868, when the Fourteenth Amendment to the Constitution of the United States became law. In fact, the Congress in our own day continues to carry on a tradition from the past which reflects an attitude to the contrary by extending various forms of support to religion. Thus, in 1944, Congress passed the Servicemen's Readjustment Act which provided for the college and university education of those who were veterans of World War II in hundreds of religious schools and colleges and universities at the expense of the Federal government. In 1946, Congress authorized federal payments to religious schools for the purpose of providing better lunches for their pupils, and it also voted to reimburse the schools which the "pages (Congressional page-boys) may elect to attend" when their choice was a private or a parochial school.[28]

This leaves the local ordinaries of the United States, as the official and authoritative teachers in their respective dioceses, unencumbered in exercising their right and in fulfilling their obligation to the prescript of the divine law with respect to the completely Catholic religious instruction to be imparted in the Catholic uni-

---

[26] S.C.S. Off., instr., 22 aug. 1900—*Fontes*, n. 1245.

[27] Cf. Brady, *Confusion Twice Confounded, The First Amendment and the Supreme Court* (South Orange, N. J.: The Seton Hall University Press, 1954).

[28] *Ibidem*, pp. 32, 34.

versities and colleges in their territories to all attending students.

For those who allege that such a practice would lead to an aroused public opinion, would bring odium on our Catholic universities and colleges and on the Church, it is the opinion of the writer that such an assumption is based on a false notion, as false today as it was in 1882 when an observer remarked:

> "Thoughtful non-Catholic fathers have long ago consulted the best interests of their daughters and have sent them to convent-schools. They now feel forced to send their sons to our Catholic colleges, where they are convinced that their hearts will be cultivated as well as their intellects.
>
> Our Catholic schools are to be equally staunch with the Protestant colleges. Books which are silent about the nature and the work of the Church do not suffice. It is a mockery to call a school Catholic and then use books for History or Literature from which passages assail the things so dear to the Catholic heart under the pretext of not wounding the susceptibilities of its Protestant patrons. A foolish and false notion which is wrong. It is a scandal. Every Protestant parent sending his child to a Catholic school expects to find the instruction thoroughly Catholic and, far from being pleased with the reverse, he becomes shocked to find that even in the Catholic school he meets with men who trim their very principles. Such behavior justly brings contempt on the men practicing it; unjustly also, it places the Church in a fale light. . . . We have the truth with us, and the truth shall prevail. And if our colleges cannot present it properly, then indeed they are sad failures; and far from carrying out the intention for which all the colleges and universities in Europe were originally founded and endowed, they become things of stunted growth without the energy of secular institutions and therefore, without a *raison d'être*. They are Catholic or nothing."[29]

[29] "What is the Outlook for Our Catholic Colleges"? *The American Catholic Quarterly Review,* VII (1882), 392, 400, 404, 405.

The possibility of such a hostile public opinion's emergence can be precluded, in the view of the writer, by means of the simple, effective measure of a brief explanation to the non-Catholic parents or to the non-Catholic students who come, voluntarily, to seek admittance for their children or for themelves to Catholic universities and colleges. The explanation could proceed along the following lines:

The function of a Catholic university or college is to give to its students an education which has been placed by centuries of successful effort into a definite framework. That system of education contains as a necessary part of its curriculum a course in the teachings of the Catholic Church. This need cause no concern to the non-Catholic that he will be forced to accept those teachings for his own private convictions. Rather, he is to look upon the course in Religion as an integral and valuable piece of information in the education he is to receive in a Catholic college or university. There will be no compulsion of any kind which would require the presence of the non-Catholic student at Catholic "Chapel" exercises. The classes in Religion for non-Catholic students will be a presentation of the position of the Catholic Church in matters pertaining to faith and morals, and it will serve as an intellectual contribution to the student, as an object of knowledge from the organization which always safeguards the freedom of the individual conscience.

If the matter be thus explained, there can be no valid or logical objection to the courses in the Catholic Religion required of all students in a Catholic college or university.

The current practice in some of the Catholic colleges and universities in the United States of America, which simply provides courses in the natural law for non-Catholic students[30] as substitute courses given to the Catholic students in the Catholic Religion, is not acceptable. There exists now an official and clear statement that supernatural revelation is a *moral* or *practical* necessity for an adequate knowledge of the natural law, and that this revela-

---

[30] These courses are given various names in the curricula, v.g. Fundamental Principles of Morality; Foundations of Natural Religion; Natural Ethics.

tion has been entrusted to the Church to be preserved and explained along with the natural law.

> "Disagreement and error among men on moral and religious matters have always been a cause of profound sorrow to all good men, but above all to the true and loyal sons of the Church, especially today, when we see the principles of Christian culture being attacked on all sides.
>
> It is not surprising that such discord and error should always have existed outside the fold of Christ. For though, absolutely speaking, human reason by its own natural force and light can arrive at a true and certain knowledge of the one personal God, Who by His providence watches over and governs the world, and also of the natural law, which the Creator has written in our hearts, still there are not a few obstacles to prevent reason from making efficient and fruitful use of its natural ability. The truths that have to do with God and the relations between God and men completely surpass the sensible order and demand self-surrender and self-abnegation in order to be put into practice and to influence practical life. Now the human intellect, in gaining the knowledge of such truths is hampered both by the activity of the senses and the imagination, and by evil passions arising from original sin. Hence men easily persuade themselves in such matters that what they do not wish to believe is false or at least doubtful.
>
> It is for this reason that divine relevation must be considered morally necessary, so that those religious and moral truths which are not of their nature beyond the reach of reason in the present condition of the human race may be known by all men readily with a firm certainty and with freedom from all error."[31]

The teaching of the Church, then, is a practical necessity for a knowledge of the natural law which will be free from error as

[31] Pius XII, Ep. encycl. *Humani generis,* 12 aug. 1950—*AAS,* XLII (1950), 561, 562 (Translation by the National Catholic Welfare Conference).

to the existence or the extent of certain obligations. To teach the natural law apart from Catholic doctrine to non-Catholics while giving instruction and education in the Catholic Religion to Catholic students is to teach two objective standards of morality, one for Catholics and one for non-Catholics. This can only lead to Indifferentism. There can be no place in the curriculum of an American Catholic university or college for "electives" in some other field of knowledge as a substitute offered to non-Catholic students for courses in the Catholic Religion, even though that field be philosophy or sociology. Much less can there be accorded a "complete academic freedom" to the non-Catholic students with reference to a study of Caholic teaching. Pope Pius XI quoted a layman who wrote: "The school, if not a temple is a den. When literary, social, domestic and religous education do not go hand in hand, man is unhappy and helpless."[32]

[32] Pius XI, Ep. encycl. *Divini illius Magistri,* 31 dec. 1929—*AAS*, XXII (1930), 76.

CONCLUSIONS

1. The term *pueri* as chosen by the codifiers of the Code of Canon Law was indefinite and generic in its meaning in the pre-Code law, and it embraced students on all levels of education.

2. The term *pueri* as used by the legislator in canon 1374 makes the prohibition of that canon applicable to all Catholic youth who are still in the process of acquiring a formal education, i.e., to all those who are to be instructed in elementary schools, high-schools, colleges and universities.

3. The toleration mentioned in canon 1374 is not to be confused with tolerance, which conveys the idea of an attitude or a habitual state of the mind, and leaves the impression that the Church permits and condones the attendance of Catholics at universities or colleges of a neutral or mixed character.

4. When local ordinaries are empowered to concede a negative toleration of this evil, this is not to be construed as a consent or an approval that replaces their opposition to the evil or supplants their desire for its removal.

5. When the local ordinary has determined that a particular procedure is to be followed by his subjects in the matter of securing the toleration for attendance at universities or colleges of a neutral or mixed character, his particular law is alike to be observed by boarding and non-boarding travelers or strangers (*peregrini*).

6. An exempt priest religious seeking to attend a secular university is required to seek the express permission of the local ordinary of the territory wherein the secular university is situated when such a procedure is for the sake of the common good required of all who attend that university.

7. As non-exempt religious, all women religious are subject to the jurisdiction of the local ordinary in the matter of attendance at universities or colleges of a neutral or mixed character, unless an indult makes other provisions.

8. When the local ordinary deems a prudent silence, rather than a decree of toleration, to be the wise, temporary solution in the matter of the attendance of Catholics at universities or colleges of a neutral or mixed character, pastors and other priests may offer a prudent judgment in individual cases, which however does not impose any strictly canonical obligation on the students or their parents.

9. The III Plenary Council of Baltimore (1884) left the judgment concerning the attendance of Catholics at universities or colleges of a neutral or mixed character to the parents when it was found that a desired course of study was not offered by Catholic univerities or colleges. Since the particular law of the Council permitted that which is prohibited in the universal law of the Code, that law is abrogated.

10. Although a mathematical proportion for the number of non-Catholic students who may be admitted to Catholic universities and colleges has not been given by the Holy See, it is submitted by the writer that a proportion of non-Catholic students to the measure of one-third of the entire student body in any Catholic university or college will, ordinarily, place that university or college in the danger of losing its nature and its power of influence as a truly Catholic university or college.

11. The current practice in some of the Catholic universities and colleges in the United States, which simply provides courses in the natural law for non-Catholics as substitutes for the courses given to the Catholic students in the Catholic Religion, is not an acceptable mode of procedure.

BIBLIOGRAPHY

Sources

Acta Apostolicae Sedis, Commentarium Officiale, Romae, 1909.

Acta et Decreta Concilii Plenarii Baltimorensis Tertii, A. D. MDCCCLXXXIV, Baltimorae: John Murphy, 1886.

Acta et Decreta Sacrorum Conciliorum Recentiorum, Collectio Lacensis, 7 vols., Friburgi Brisgoviae, 1870-1892.

Acta Sanctae Sedis, 41 vols., Romae, 1865-1908.

Acta Sanctorum, quotquot toto orbe coluntur, vel a catholicis scriptoribus celebrantur quae ex latinis et graecis, aliarumque gentium antiquis monumentis collegit, digessit, notis illustravit Joannes Bolandus . . . servata primigenia scriptorum phrasi. Operum et studium contulit Godefridus Henschenius . . . Edito novissima, curante Joannes Carnondet, 71 vols., Parisiis: V. Palmé, 1863-1940.

Bouscaren, T. Lincoln, *The Canon Law Digest,* 3 vols. and Supplements through 1953 and 1954, Milwaukee: Bruce & Co., 1934-1949-1953-1954-1955.

Codex Iuris Canonici, Pii X Pontificis Maximi iussu digestus, Benedicti Papae XV auctoritate promulgatus, Praefatione, Fontium Annotatione et Indice Analytico-Alphabetico, ab Emo Petri Card. Gasparri Auctus, Romae: Typis Polyglottis Vaticanis, 1917; Reimpressio, 1934.

Cadicis Iuris Canonici Fontes, cura Emi Petri Card. Gasparri editi, 9 vols., Romae (postea Civitate Vaticana): Typis Polyglottis Vaticanis, 1923-1939 (Vols. VII-IX, ed. cura et studio Emi. Iustiniani Card, Serédi).

Collectanea Sacrae Congregationis de Propaganda Fide, 2 vols. (Vol. I, Ann. 1622-1866, Nn. 1-1299; Vol. II, Ann. 1867-1906, Nn. 1300-2317), Romae: Typographia Polyglotta, 1907.

Corpus Iuris Civilis, 3 vols., Vol. I, *Institutiones,* quas recognovit P. Krueger; *Digesta,* quae recognovit T. Mommsen et retractavit P. Krueger, ed. stereotypa 15., Berolini: Apud Weidmannos, 1928.

Decretales D. Gregorii Papae IX, una cum glossis, Romae, 1582.

Denzinger, H.-Umberg, J., *Enchirdion Symbolorum Definitionum et Declarationum de Rebus Fidei et Morum,* editio vigesima sexta, emendata et aucta, Friburgi Brisgoviae: Herder and Co., 1947.

Hardouin, J., *Acta Conciliorum et Epistolae Decretales ac Constitutiones Summorum Pontificum,* 12 vols., Parisiis, 1715.

Leonis XIII, Pontificis Maximi, Acta, 23 vols., Romae: Typographica Vaticana, 1881-1905.

Liber Sextus Decretalium D. Bonifacii Papae VIII, suae integritati cum Clementinis et Extravagantibus, earumque Glossis restitutis, Romae, 1582.

Mansi, J. D., *Sacrorum Conciliorum Nova et Amplissima Collectio,* 53 vols. in 59, Parisiis, Arnhemii, Lipsiae, 1901-1927.

Monumenta Germaniae Historica, Scriptores, Inde ab Anno Christi, Quingentesimo usque ad Annum Millesimum et Quingentesimum, Tom. XXIII, ed. Georgius Henricus Pertz, Hannoverae, 1874.

New Testament of Our Lord and Savior Jesus Christ, The, The Episcopal Committee of the Confraternity of Christian Doctrine, Paterson, N. J.: St. Anthony's Guild Press, 1941.

Schroeder, H. J., *Canons and Decrees of the Council of Trent: Original Text with English Translation,* St. Louis: B. Herder Book Co. 1941.

Reference Works

Adams, Henry B., *Thomas Jefferson and the University of Virginia,* Washington, D. C.: Government Printing Office, 1888.

Anstey, Harold, *Munimenta Academica,* or Documents illustrative of academical life and studies at Oxford. . . .Published by the authority of the Lords Commissioners of Her Majesty's Treasury, under the direction of the Master of the Rolls, 2 vols., London: Longmans, Green, Reader and Dyer, 1868.

Augustine, Charles, *A Commentary on the New Code of Canon Law,* 8 vols., Vol. I, 5. ed., St. Louis: Herder & Co., 1926.

Ayrinhac, H. A.-Lydon, P. J., *Penal Legislation in the New Code of Canon Law,* rev. ed., New York: Benziger Bros., 1936.

Bell, Bernard I., *The Crisis in Education,* New York: Whittlesey House, 1949.

Berger, Adolph, *Encyclopedic Dictionary of Roman Law,* Philadelphia: The American Philosophical Society, 1953.

Beste, Udalricus, *Introductio in Codicem,* 3. ed. Collegeville, Minn.: St. John's Abbey Press, 1946.

Blat, Albertus, *Commentarium Textus Codicis Iuris Canonici,* 6 vols., Romae: Collegio Angelico, 1919-1927.

Boffa, C., *Canonical Provisions for Catholic Schools (Elementary and Intermediate),* The Catholic University of America Canon Law Studies, n. 117, Washington, D. C.: The Catholic University of America Press, 1939.

Bouscaren, T. L.-Ellis, A. C., *Canon Law, A Text and Commentary,* 2. ed., Milwaukee: Bruce and Co. 1951.

Brady, Joseph, *Confusion Twice Confounded, The First Amendment and the Supreme Court,* South Orange, N. J.: The Seton Hall University Press, 1954.

Brooks, Phillips, *The Oldest School in America,* Boston and New York: Houghton, Mifflin & Co., 1885.

Burns, James A., *The Catholic School System in the United States,* New York: Benziger Bros; 1908.

Cappello, Felix M., *De Censuris,* Taurini: Marietti, 1925.

——— *Summa Iuris Publici Ecclesiastici,* 2. ed., Romae: Apud Aedes Universitatis Gregorianae, 1929.

Casey, James, *A Study of Canon 2222, § 1,* The Catholic University of America Canon Law Studies, n. 290, Washington, D. C.: The Catholic University of America Press, 1949.

Cassidy, Francis P., *Catholic College Foundations and Development in the United States* (1677-1850), Washington, D. C., 1924.

Catholic Encyclopedia, The, 15 vols., Index and Supplement, New York: 1907-1922.

Cicognani, Amleto, *Canon Law,* 2. rev. ed., authorized English version by O'Hara & Brennan, Philadelphia: The Dolphin Press, 1935; reprinted Westminster, Md.: The Newman Press, 1949.

Clarke, Robert H., *Lives of the Deceased Bishops of the Catholic Church in the United States,* 2 vols., New York: P. O'Shea, 1872.

Commager, Henry S., *Documents of American History,* 5. ed., New York: Appleton, Century-Crofts, Inc., 1940.

Coronata, Matthaeus Conte a, *Institutiones Iuris Canonici,* 5 vols., Vol. II, 4. ed., Taurini: Marietti, 1951.

Costello, John *Domicile and Quasi-Domicile,* The Catholic University of America Canon Law Studies, n. 60, The Catholic University of America, 1930.

Creusen, Joseph, *Religious Men and Women in the Code,* 5. ed., revised and edited by A. C. Ellis, Milwaukee: Bruce Publishing Co., 1953.

Damman, Mother Grace, *Essays on Catholic Education,* Washington, D. C.: The Catholic University of America Press, 1942.

De Hovre, R., *Philosophy and Education,* trans. by E. Jordan, New York: Benziger Bros., 1931.

De Meester, Alphonsus, *Juris Canonici et Juris Canonico-Civilis Compendium,* nova ed., 3 vols. in 4, Brugis: Descleé, De Brouwer, 1921-1928.

Denifle, Heinrich, *Die Entstehung der Universitäten des Mittelalters bis 1400,* Berlin: Weidmann Buchhandlung, 1855.

——— *Archiv für Literatur und Kirchengeschichte,* 7 vols., Berlin: 1885-1900.

——— Chatelain, A., *Chartularium Universitatis Parisiensis.* Sub auspiciis Consilii Generalis Facultatum Parisiensium ex diversis bibliothecis tabulariisque collegit et cum authenticis chartis contulit Henricus Denifle . . . auxiliante . . . Aemilio Chatelain, 4 vols., Parisiis: 1889-1897.

Discorsi e Radiomessagi di Sua Santità, Pio XII, 15 vols. to 1955, Romae: Tipografia Poliglotta Vaticana, 1939—

Ernout, Alfred, *Plaute,* 7 vols., Paris: Société D'Edition "Les Belles Lettres," 1932-1940.

Ford, Wm. C., *The Writings of John Adams,* 7 vols., New York: The Macmillan Co., 1913-1917.

Frazer, Sir James, *The Fasti of Ovid,* 5 vols., London: Macmillan & Co., 1929.

Gasparri, P. Card., *Schema Codicis Iuris Canonici,* Libri I, II (1912), III, V (1913), IV (1914), Romae: Typis Polyglottis Vaticanis.

Gibson, Stanley, *Statuta Antiqua Universitatis Oxoniensis,* Oxford: The Clarendon Press, 1931.

Graves, Frank, *History of Education during the Middle Ages,* New York: The Macmillan Co., 1910.

Gross, Henry, *The Gild-Merchant,* Oxford: The Clarendon Press, 1890.

Giulday, Peter, *The Life and Times of John Carroll,* New York: The Encyclopedia Press, 1922.

——— *The National Pastorals of the American Hierarchy,* Washington, D. C., 1923.

Hammill, John, *The Obligations of the Traveler According to Canon 14,* The Catholic University of America Canon Law Studies, n. 160, Washington, D. C.: The Catholic University of America Press, 1942.

Hartfelder, Karl, *Philip Melanchthon, Praeceptor Germaniae,* Berlin: A. Hoffman, 1889.

Hill, Wm. H., *Historical Sketches of the St. Louis University,* St. Louis: P. Fox, 1879.

Hostiensis, Cardinalis (Henricus de Segusio), *In Decretalium Libros Commentaria,* 5 vols. in 3, Venetiis, 1581.

Hughes, T., *Loyola and the Educational System of the Jesuits,* New York: Chas. Scribner's Sons, 1892.

Huillard-Breholles, Jean L., *Historia Diplomatica Frederici II,* sive, Constitutiones, Privilegia, Mandata, Instrumenta quae supersunt istius imperatoris et filiorum eius. Accedunt epistolae paparum et documenta varia. Collegit, ad fidem cartarum et codicum recensuit, iuxta seriem annorum disposuit et notis illustravit. Auspiciis et sumptibus H. de Albertis de Luynes . . . 7 vols. in 12, Parisiis: excudebant Plon Fratres, 1852-1861.

Jone, Heribert, *Commentarium in Codicem Iuris Canonici,* 3 vols., I (1950), II (1954), III (1955), Paderborn: Fred. Schöningh.

Kane, Wm., *An Essay toward a History of Education,* Chicago: Loyola University Press, 1935.

Kearney, Raymond, *The Principles of Delegation,* The Catholic University of America Canon Law Studies, n. 55, Washington, D. C.: The Catholic University of America, 1929.

Keene, Michael, *Religious Ordinaries and Canon 198,* The Catholic University of America Canon Law Studies, n. 135, Washington, D. C.; The Catholic University of America Press, 1942.

Leach, Arthur F., *English Schools at the Reformation,* Westminster: A. Constable & Co., 1896.

Locke, John, *An Essay Concerning Human Understanding,* London: J. F. Dove, 1828.

——— *Thoughts Concerning Education,* ed. by R. H. Quick, London: Cambridge University Press. C. J. Clay & Sons, 1892.

Magevney, Eugene A., *The Reformation and Education,* New York: The Cathedral Library Association, 1903.

Massachusetts Historical Society, *Proceedings,* Boston: The Society, 1859-19—.

1 Sec., Vols. 1-20; 1791/1835—1882/83

2 Sec., Vols. 1-20; 1884/1885—1906/07

3 Sec., Vols. 41-60; 1907/08—Oct. 1926/June 1927.

McCormick, P. J. and Cassidy, F. P., *History of Education,* Washington, D. C.: The Catholic Education Press, 1953.

Memorial Volume of the Centenary of St. Mary's Seminary of St. Sulpice, Baltimore, Md., 1891.

Meyer, Theo., *Institutiones Iuris Naturalis,* 2 vols., Friburgi Brisgoviae, 1900.

Michiels, Gommarus, *Normae Generales Iuris Canonici,* 2. ed., 2 vols., Parisiis-Tournai-Romae: Descleé, 1949.

Migne, P. J., *Patrologiae Cursus Completus, Series Latina,* 221 vols., Parisiis: 1844-1864.

Montgomery, Thos. H., *A History of the University of Pennsylvania, 1749-1770,* Philadelphia: G. W. Jacobs & Co., 1900.

Moore, Edward C., *The Story of Instruction,* New York: The Macmillan Company, 1938.

Mörsdorf, Klaus, *Die Rechtssprache des Codex Iuris Canonici,* Paderborn: Fred. Schöningh, 1937.

Neuberger, Nicholas, *Canon 6 or the Relation of the Codex Iuris Canonici to Preceding Legislation,* The Cathodic University of America Canon Law Studies, n. 44, Washington, D. C.: The Catholic University of America, 1927.

Newman Club in American Education, The, Washington, D. C.: The National Association of Newman Club Chaplains, 1953.

Newman Club Manual, Washington, D. C.: The National Newman Club Federation, 1953.

Official Catholic Directory, The, New York: P. J. Kenedy & Sons, 1955.

Ottaviani, Alafridus, *Institutiones Iuris Publici Ecclesiastici,* 3. ed., 2 vols., Romae: Typis Polyglottis Vaticanis, 1947-1948.

Paulsen, Fred., *The German Universities and University Study,* trans. by F. Thilly, New York: Chas. Scribner's Sons, 1906.

——— *German Education, Past and Present,* trans. by T. Lorenz, New York: Chas. Scribner's Sons, 1908.

Pejška, Josephus, *Ius Canonicum Religiosorum,* 3. ed. Friburgi Brisgoviae: Herder & Co., 1927.

Prümmer, Dominicus, *Manuale Iuris Canonici,* 4. ed., Friburgi: Herder, 1927.

Quincy, Josiah, *A History of Harvard University,* 2 vols., Cambridge: J. Owen, 1840.

Rashdall, Hastings, *The Universities of Europe in the Middle Ages,* 3 vols., ed. by F. M. Powicke and A. B. Emden, Oxford: The Clarendon Press, 1936.

Regatillo, E., *Institutiones Iuris Canonici,* 2 vols., Santander: Sal Terrae, 1942.

Reiffenstuel, Anacletus, *Ius Canonicum Universum,* 7 vols., ed. by V. Pelletier, Parisiis, 1864-1870.

Reilly, Thos., *The Visitation of Religious,* The Catholic University of America Canon Law Studies, n. 112, Washington, D. C.: The Catholic University of America, 1938.

Ryan, Gerald, *Principles of Episcopal Jurisdiction,* The Catholic University of America Canon Law Studies, n. 120, The Catholic University of America Press, 1939.

Salter, Harold, *Medieval Archives of the University of Oxford,* 2 vols., Oxford: The Clarendon Press, 1917-1919.

Sarti, Maurus, *De claris Archgymnasii Bononiensis Professoribus a Saeculo XI, usque ad Saeculum XIV,* 2 vols., Bononiae: Ex Typographia Laelii a Vulpe, Instituti Scientiarum Typographi, 1769-1772—completed by M. Fattorini after Sarti's death.

Savigny, F. C. von, *Geschichte des römischen Rechts im Mittelalter,* 2. ed., 7 vols., Heidelberg: J. C. B. Mohr, 1834-1851; Nachdruck, 1934-1935.

Schroeder, H. J., *Disciplinary Decrees of the General Councils,* St. Louis: B. Herder & Co., 1937.

Schwickerath, R., *Jesuit Education: Its History and Principles in the Light of Modern Educational Problems,* St. Louis: B. Herder Book Co., 1904.

Shea, John G., *History of Georgetown College,* New York: P. F. Collier, 1891.

——— *History of the Catholic Church in the United States,* 4 vols., Akron, Ohio: D. H. McBride & Co., 1886-1892.

Slafkosky, Andrew, *The Canonical Episcopal Visitation of the Diocese,* The Catholic University of America Canon Law Studies, n. 142, Washington, D. C.: The Catholic University of America Press, 1941. Salesiani, 1950.

Stickler, A. M., *Historia Iuris Canonici Latini*, I, *Historia Fontium*, Augustae Taurinorum: Apud Custodiam Librariam Pontif. Athenaei

Swoboda, Innocent, *Ignorance in Relation to the Imputability of Delicts*, The Catholic University of America Canon Law Studies, n. 143, Washington, D. C.: The Catholic University of America Press, 1941.

Thomas Aquinas, St., *Quaestiones Disputatae*, Vol. I, *De Veritate*, cura et studio P. Fr. Raymundi Spiazzi, O.P., 8. ed. revisa, Taurini-Romae: Marietti, 1949.

Thwing, Chas., *A History of Higher Education in America*, New York: D. Appleton & Co., 1906.

Treacy, Wm. P., *Old Catholic Maryland and Its Early Jesuit Missionaries*, Swedesboro, N. J., 1899.

Treaty and Concordat Between the Holy See and Italy, 2. printing, Washington, D. C.: National Catholic Welfare Conference, 1929.

Tschuppik, Karl, *Francis Joseph I, The Downfall of an Empire*, trans. by C. J. S. Sprigge, New York: Harcourt, Brace & Co., 1930.

Tyrell, R.-Pruser, C., *The Correspondence of M. Tullius Cicero*, 7 vols., London: Longmans, Green & Co., 1886-1901.

Van Hove, A., *Commentarium Lovaniense in Codicem Iuris Canonici*, 1 vol. in 5 tomes, Tom. II, *De Legibus Ecclesiasticis*, 1930; Tom. V, *De Privilegiis et Dispensationibus*, 1939, Mechliniae-Romae: H. Dessain.

Vermeersch, A.-Creusen, J., *Epitome Iuris Canonici*, 3 vols., Vol. II, 7. ed., Mechliniae-Romae: H. Dessain, 1954.

Wernz, Franciscus, *Ius Decretalium*, 6 vols., Vol. I, 1898, Vol. III, 1901, Vol. VI, 1913, Romae et Prati.

——— Vidal, P., *Ius Canonicum ad Codicis Normam Exactum*, 7 Tomes in 8 vols., Tom. IV, Vol. II, Romae: Apud Aedes Universitatis Gregorianae, 1935.

Winthrop, Robert, *Life and Letters of John Winthrop*, 2 vols., Boston: Ticknor and Fields, 1846-1867.

Woywod, S.-Smith, E., *A Practical Commentary on the Code of Canon Law*, rev. ed. 2 vols., New York: J. F. Wagner, Inc., 1948.

Articles

Anon.—"What is the Outlook for Our Colleges"? *The American Catholic Quarterly Review*, VII (1882), 385-407.

Bender, L., "Dubium Iuris in Canone 15," *Ephemerides Iuris Canonici*, XI (1955), 9-27.

Guay, A., "Fréquentation des Écoles Non-Catholiques," *Revue de l'Université d'Ottawa*, VII (1937), 33*-59*.

Heuser, H. J., "Prince Bismarck's Conflict with the Catholic Church," *The American Catholic Quarterly Review*, IX (1884), 322-339.

Maguire, J., "Another Look at Subversion of Faith," *America*, Vol. XCII, No. 10 (Dec. 4, 1954), 269-271.

Nilles, N., "Tolerari Potest," *Zeitschrift für katholische Theologie,* XVII (1892), 247-274.

Roelker, E., "The Traveler and Local Statutes," *The Jurist,* II (1942), 110-115.

Schmidt, J. R., "The Juridic Value of the *Instructio,*" *The Jurist,* I (1941), 289-316.

Tabera, J., "Annotationes," *Commentarium pro Religiosis et Missionariis,* XXIV (1943), 3-6.

Toscanel, P., "Annotationes ad Monitum S. Officii de Associationibus communisticis puerorum," *Apollinaris,* XXIII (1950), 266-276.

Vermeersch, A., "Quinam sunt Pueri de Quibus in Can. 1373, § 1, et 1374"? *Periodica,* XVII (1928), 145*-148*.

PERIODICALS

America, National Catholic Weekly Review, New York, 1909—

American Catholic Quarterly Review, The, Philadelphia, 1876-1923.

Apollinaris, Romae, 1928—

Catholic Documents, London, 1950—

Commentarium pro Religiosis et Missionariis, Romae, 1920—

Ephemerides Iuris Canonici, Romae, 1945—

Jurist, The, Washington, D. C., 1941—

Periodica de Religiosis et Missionariis, Brugis, 1905-1919; ab anno 1920; *Periodica de Re Canonica et Morali utilia praesertim Religiosis et Missionariis,* Brugis, 1920-1927; *Periodica de Re Morali, Canonica, Liturgica,* Brugis, 1927-1936, et Romae, 1937—

Revue de l'Université d'Ottawa, Ottawa, 1931—

Time, The Weekly News Magazine, New York, 1923—

Zeitschrift für katholische Theologie, Innsbruck, 1877—

ALPHABETICAL INDEX

Abbot Desiderius, 5
Abbot of St. Remy, 72
Abelard, 12
Academy of Arts and Sciences, 38
Adam of St. Victor, 12
Adams, John, 38
Anglicanism, 33, 44, 45
Annual Statement of the Bishops of America (1954), 125
Archbishop of Frieburg, Letter of Pius IX to the, 50
Archdeacon, The, 11, 12, 13
Austria, Pius IX to the Bishops of, 49, 50
  Leo XIII and Non-Catholics at Catholic schools in, 55
Authentic Interpretation of the Code, 70

Belgium, Leo XIII's opposition to civil law on education in, 53, 54
Boston Latin School, The, 37
Bruno, St., 7

Carroll, Bishop John, 21
  Pastoral Letter of, 56, 57
Catholic University of America, The, 28
Chancellor, The, 11, 12, 13, 15
Cicero, The Meaning of *pueri* in, 72
Circumstances permitting a Decree of Toleration, 137, 138
Clerics,
  and attendance at secular universities, 45, 46, 105, 106
  and the Letter of Cardinal Gasparri on attendance at secular universities, 108, 109
  who are exempt, 107, 114
Colleges in the United States,
  Origins of Catholic, 17
    Georgetown, 20
    Newtown, 20
    Notre Dame, 23
    St. Elizabeth's, 23
    St. Louis, 23
    St. Mary's, 22
    Trinity, 23
  Origins of Non-Catholic.
    Harvard, 36
    Bryn Mawr, 40
    Smith, 40
    Vassar, 40
    Wellesley, 40
    William and Mary, 39
Collegium, The meaning of, 4
  Constantinople, 17
  Sorbonne, 17
Commission of Reform, The, 25
Concordats and canonical vigilance and visitation by local ordinaries, 115, 116, 117, 118
Conscience,
  Exhortation of Poux XII for the education of, 130
  Necessity for the education of, 128, 129
  Sources for the education of, 128, 129
Constantinus Africanus, 5
Corpus Iuris Civilis, The, 8
Council of,
  Augsburg, 43, 73
  Cologne, 43
  Constance, 41
  III Lateran, 13
  IV Lateran, 13
  V Lateran, 41, 72
  I Plen. Balt., 59
  II Plen. Balt., 50
  III Plen. Balt., 28, 44, 75, 135, 144
  I Prov. Balt., 57
  II Prov. Balt., 58
  IV Prov. Balt., 58
  Trent, 27, 42, 44
  Vatican, 61, 98
Crudades, The, 3

Deans, 13
Decree of Toleration, The,
  by the local ordinary or his delegates, 139

Degrees,
Bachelor, Licentiate, Doctorate, 14
Length of time of required studies for, 14, 25
Delegation,
by the local ordinary, 119
Canonical concept of, 118
Determinatio, The, 15
Digesta, The, 8
Dissimulatio, 89
Dolus,
necessary for the incurring of excommunication, 85
Domicile,
The subject of a particular ordinary by reason of, 97, 98, 99
Doubt, St. Thomas on, 6, 9
Dubium iuris and the prohibition of canon 1374, 68, 69, 70

Education,
Bernard Iddings Bells on Religious, 125
Catholic Church in, 82, 83, 145, 146
John Sloan Dickey on Religious, 124
Leo XIII on, and harmony with Catholic Faith, 53
Nathan M. Pusey on Religious, 124
of the human conscience in statements of Pope Pius XII, 126, 127, 128, 129
Norms of Pius IX for Catholic, 52, 53
Pius XI and the necessity of Religious, 81, 82
Proper and immediate end of, 81, 82
Religious, during the Reformation, 44
Religious, in American private and non sectarian universities and colleges, 121, 122, 123, 124
Religious, in years of higher studies in statements of Pius XII, 118, 126, 127
Religious, of Non-Catholics in Catholic universities and colleges, 159, 160
The highest duty of, in statement of Pius XII, 129
White House Conference on, 124
Edward VI, King, 33
Elizabeth, Queen, 33
England, Leo XIII's solution to problems in, 54
Excommunication,
Classes of people who may incur, 84, 85
Conditions for the incurring of, 85

Fourteenth Amendment,The, 159
France, Leo XIII's position on religion in education in, 54
Franklin, Benjamin, 37
Frederick II, Emperor, 6

Galen, 6
Germany,
Pius IX's condemnation of neutral schools in, 50
Leo's XIII and Non-Catholics at Catholic schools in, 55
Glossae, 10
Gratian,
Canon Law separated from Theology by, 8
Decretum of, 8, 9, 10
Guido, St., 7
Guiscard, Robert, 5
Gymnasia, 43

Harvard, John, 36
Harvard College and its early course of studies, 36
Henry VIII, King, 33
Hippocrates, Aphorisms of, 3
Hostiensis, the meaning of *pueri* in, 72
Hugh of St. Victor, 12
Hungary, Leo XIII's instructions to the Bishops of, 54, 55
Hus, John, 41

Imperium in the Church, 95
Inceptio, The, 13
Instructions of the Holy See, The, as norms for local ordinaries, 133, 134
Canonical force of, 71, 136, 152, 153
Nature of, 71, 120, 135
Intellectuals, The duties of, 128
International Institute, The, 38
Irnerius, 8
Italy, Pius IX to the Bishops of, 48

Jefferson, Thomas, and the purposes of higher education, 38, 39
Jesuits, The, 22, 23, 27, 35

Jurisdiction, Ecclesiastical,
Concept of, 95, 96, 97
Formal object of, 101
Subjects of, 97

Licentia Docendi, The, 11, 13, 24
Local Ordinary, The,
and circumstances in his territory, 137, 138
and coercive power in his territory, 86, 87
and his obligation to issue a Decree of Toleration, 143
and the Instructions of the Holy See, 133, 134
and limitations of his jurisdiction, 96, 97
and safeguards, 138, 139
and Vigilance and Visitation, 112
as official teacher in his territory, 148, 149
persons so considered, 93, 94
The Decree of Toleration of, 139
Locke, John, and his aim in Education, 34
Lombard League, The 7

Magisterium in the Church, 95, 147
Massachusetts Colony, The, 35, 36
Master-University, The, 13
Matricula, The, 10
Monte Cassino, Abbey of, 5

Nations in the early universities, 16, 18
Natural Law, The,
Necessity of Revelation for the correct knowledge of, 162, 163
Teaching of, to Non-Catholics in Catholic Universities and Colleges, 161, 162, 163
New Morality, The, 130
Non-Catholics in Catholic Universities and Colleges,
Determination of policy concerning, 150, 151
Proportionate number to be admitted, 152, 154, 156
Non-Catholic Universities and Colleges,
Acatholica, 79
Mixta, 80
Neutra, 79
Dangers from, 81, 82, 132
Ordinance of 1787, The, 38

Oriental Rite, The
Bishops of, 73, 74
Catholics of, 74
Ovid, the meaning of *pueri* in, 72

Parents,
Leo XIII to, on the education of youth, 62, 63
Right of choice of university or college for children, 82, 83
Subject to excommunication, 84, 85
Pastoral Letters of the American Bishops, The,
1792, 55, 56
1833, 1840, 58
1844, 61, 62, 135
Pastors,
and other priests, and their judgment in matters of attendance at non-Catholic universities and colleges, 144
Penalties,
Those which the local ordinary may enact, 87
Peregrini,
as subjects of the local ordinary, 99
in Canon Law, 98
Title of authority over, 102
Physical Culture in statement of Pius XII, 141, 142
Plautus, the meaning of *pueri* in, 72
Poland, Leo XII's condemnation of certain schools in, 55
Pole, Cardinal, 25
Pontificial Commission for the Authentic Interruption of the Code, The, 70, 136
Pope,
Alexander II, 24
Boniface VIII, 25
Gregory IX, 72
Honorius III, 9, 11, 25
Innocent III, 17
Innocent IV, 18
Leo XIII, 28, 53, 55
Nicholas IV, 11
Pius V, 135
Pius IX, 27, 46, 48, 50
Pius XI, 28, 67, 81, 120, 163
Pius XII, 29, 119, 121, 125, 128, 141
St. Pius X, 75, 105, 136
Victor III, 5
Principium, The, 13
Prohibition of Canon 1374, The, 67, 68
and the III Plenary Council of Baltimore, 144

Public Order,
and the power of the local ordinary, 104
as distinct from the public good, 103
Juridical Concept of, The, 102
Pueri,
Extension of to embrace those eligible for attendance at universities and colleges, 70
in Roman Law, 72
Juridical meaning of, The, 71, 74, 76, 77, 78
Usual meaning of, The, 75
Puritans, The, 33

Quasi-Domicile, The subject of a particular ordinary by reason of, 92, 99

Rector, The, 13
Reformation, The Protestant, 19, 25, 30, 33, 44, 45
and effects on education, 30, 45, 79
Regimen, the social power in the Church, 94
Reiffenstuel, the meaning of *pueri* in, 72
Religious Peace of Augsburg, The, 44
Revolution, The French, 22, 45
Robert de Courçon, 14
Royal License, The, 6

Sacred Congregation,
of Bishops and Regulars on attendance at secular universities by clerics, 105
Consistorial, and attendance at secular universities by clerics, 105, 106
for the Propagation of the Faith,
Norms for China, 55, 73, 74
Norms for Ireland, 46, 47, 48, 73
Norms for Missionaries, 73
Number of Non-Catholics to be admitted to Catholic Universities and Colleges, 154
of the Holy Office,
Communistic Organizations and Schools, 80
Masonic Influence in Education, 75
Norms for the East Indies, 52
Norms for England, 51
Norms for Oriental Bishops, 52
Norms for Syria, 51, 52
Norms for Switzerland, 51, 74
Proportionate number of non-Catholics to be admitted to Catholic schools, 153, 154
Religious instruction of Non-Catholics in Catholic schools, 158, 159
Safeguards required before a Decree of Toleration, 138, 159
Sardinia, Pius IX to the Bishops of, 48, 49
Sercicemen's Readjustment Act of 1944, The, 159
Sicily, Pius IX to the Bishops of, 49
Spain, Pius IX to the Bishops of, 49
Statutes of the German Guild of Students, The, 9
Stephen of Lexington, 17
Stephen of Tournay, 12
Student-Guilds, The, 9
Student-University, The, 9
Studium Generale, The, 4, 5, 15
St. Louis IX, King, 18
St. Sulpice, The Society of, 20, 22
Syllabus of Pius IX, The, 50
Switzerland,
Leo XIII and attendance of Non-Catholics at Catholic schools in, 55
Technical Universities and Colleges, 80, 81
Tolerance, 92
Toleration,
different from *dissimulatio*, 89
in matters of positive human law, 91
in matters of the natural law, 91
juridice sense of, The, 91
Tacit or Express, 92, 143
usual meaning of, The, 89, 90
Toynbee, Arnold,
Concept of Christianity and Revelation, 125
Treaty of Constance, The, 7

Universitas, The meaning of, 2, 3, 4
Universities,
function of the modern, The, 131, 132
Number of in the middle Ages, 19, 24
Number of during the Reformation, 27
University growth, 17, 18, 19
in England, 33
in Germany, 31

University of, The,
  Berlin, 32
  Bologna, 7
    Method of teaching at, 10
    Process of graduation at, 10
  Cologne, 45
  Montpelier, 7
  Oxford, 15, 74
    Courses of study at, 16, 17
  Paris, 12
  Pennsylvania, 37
  Salerno, 5, 6
  Utrecht, 45
  Virginia, 39

Vigilance, 112
  as distinct from Visitation, 113
Virginia Colony, The, 35
Visitation, Canonical, 113, 114

Walter of St. Victor, 12
William of Champaux, 12
Winthrop, John, and Catholic Education in America, 35
Women Religious and the local ordinary, 110, 111
Women and their early higher education in America, 40
Wycliff, John, 41

BIOGRAPHICAL NOTE

ALEXANDER F. SOKOLICH was born on August 14, 1918, in Somerville, New Jersey. He received his elementary and the first two years of his high school education in the Jersey City Public Schools. In 1935 he entered Seton Hall Preparatory School, South Orange, New Jersey, from which he was graduated in June, 1937. In that same year he entered Seton Hall College, South Orange, New Jersey. In July 1939, he began the course in Scholastic Philosophy at Immaculate Conception Seminary, Darlington, New Jersey. He received the degree of Bachelor of Arts from Seton Hall College in June of 1941. In September of 1941 he began the study of the Sacred Sciences at Immaculate Conception Seminary, Darlington, New Jersey, and in 1944 entered Theological College at the Catholic University of America, Washington, D. C. He received the degree of Licentiate in Sacred Theology from the Catholic University in 1945. He was ordained a priest for the Archdiocese of Newark on May 5, 1945. After serving as an assistant in several parishes of the Archdiocese of Newark, he enrolled in the School of Canon Law at the Catholic University of America in the fall of 1953. He received the degree of Baccalaureate in Canon Law in June, 1954, and the Licentiate in June, 1955.

CANON LAW STUDIES*

368. Bockstie, Rev. Richard, C.SS.R., J.C.L., The principal oratory of religious.
369. Grajewski, Rev. Maurice J., O.F.M., M.A., Ph.D., J.C.L., The supreme moderator of exempt religious orders.
370. Havlik, Rev. Bernard J., A.B., J.C.L., The cessation of rescripts.
371. Olkovikas, Rev. Albert William, S.T.L., J.C.L., The *instantia* of the lawsuit.
372. Poblete, Rev. Elias Olarte, J.C.L., The plenary council.
373. Sokolich, Rev. Alexander F., S.T.L., J.C.L., Canonical provisions for universities and colleges.
374. Sullivan, Rev. Jordan J., O.F.M. Cap., B.A., J.C.L., Fast and abstinence in the First Order of St. Francis.

*For a complete list of the available numbers of this series apply to the Catholic University of America Press, 620 Michigan Ave., N.E., Washington (17), D. C., for a general catalog.

www.ingramcontent.com/pod-product-compliance
Lightning Source LLC
LaVergne TN
LVHW050234080826
844660LV00012B/527
9780813225357